Betty Crocker's

Easy Mexican

MACMILLAN • USA

MACMILLAN

A Simon & Schuster Macmillan Company
1633 Broadway
New York, NY 10019

Copyright © 1995 by General Mills, Inc., Minneapolis, Minnesota

Library of Congress Cataloging-in-Publication Data

Crocker, Betty.
Betty Crocker's easy Mexican.

p. cm.

Includes index.
ISBN 0-02-860359-1

1. Cookery, Mexican.   2. Quick and easy cookery.   I. Title.
TX716.M4C758 1995

641.5972—dc20   94-42663
                                         CIP

GENERAL MILLS, INC.

Betty Crocker Food and Publications Center

Director: Marcia Copeland
Editor: Lori Fox
Recipe Development: Altanette Autry
Food Stylists: Cindy Lund and Katie McElroy

Nutrition Department
Nutritionists: Elyse A. Cohen, M.S. and Nancy Holmes, R.D.

Photographic Services
Photographer: Steve Olson

Cover by Iris Jeromnimon
Designed by Michele Laseau

Preceding page: Chili con Carne with Tomatoes (page 59)

Contents pages: Bell Pepper Nachos (page 8), Tortilla Skillet (page 44), Marinated Black-Eyed Peas (page 59),
Herbed Flank Steak (page 72), Mexican Turkey and Broccoli Salad (page 92), Mango Cream (page 104)

Front cover: Breakfast Tacos (page 32), Tortilla Skillet (page 44), Quesadillas (page 10)

Introduction

If you love Mexican food but not hard-to-find ingredients and countless hours in the kitchen, keep reading. With *Betty Crocker's Easy Mexican*, you can cook Mexican with chile-fueled fanfare but no bother.

Our recipe collection ranges freely through what we have come to know as Mexican food in America—dishes influenced by several cultures and regions, including Tex-Mex and the Southwest. From Quesadillas and Beef Burritos (there's an entire chapter on tortillas prepared in almost every way) to Spicy Turkey Burgers, our "Mexican melting pot" takes in both the traditional and the borrowed.

When you want something familiar, you'll find all the favorites, from Nifty Nachos and Chile con Queso to Chili con Carne with Tomatoes and Flan. And when you crave a new taste, there's Breakfast Tacos and Grilled Fish with Melon-Jicama Salsa. Other recipes give you the bold flavors of Mexican cooking in an unusual way—by using them in a Tex-Mex Pizza or Mexican Chicken Manicotti.

Whether tried and true or newfangled, every dish is fast and easy. And there are recipes for any occasion: speedy appetizers to serve company, a smorgasbord of salsas to perk up grilled fish or chicken, spicy casseroles to pass at a potluck supper and entrées with south-of-the-border pizzazz for great home cooking.

How can you tell a *burrito* from a *chimichanga*, or a *flauta* from an *enchilada*? Turn to our special feature on tortillas for the full story. Also, learn about selecting, storing and warming up Mexico's favorite edible wrapper.

You'll find out what to drink with your Mexican meal, too. From margaritas to coffee flavored with cinnamon, cloves and vanilla, learn what's best for putting out the fire in spicy food and ways to dress up all your cold beverages.

So when it's time for dining (or nibbling or partying) and you're in no mood for a lot of work, leaf through *Easy Mexican* for ideas. You'll find more than 120 recipes for instant hospitality with a Mexican twist.

Betty Crocker

Contents

1

Appetizers and Salsas

Sangria (page 115); Quesadillas (page 10); Snappy Stuffed Pepper (page 13)

Blue Cornmeal Chicken Wings

20 APPETIZERS

1/4 cup lime juice

1/4 cup vegetable oil

1/2 teaspoon crushed red pepper

10 chicken wings (about 2 pounds)

2 tablespoons margarine or butter

1/2 cup blue or yellow cornmeal

2 tablespoons all-purpose flour

1/2 teaspoon salt

1/2 teaspoon ground cumin

1/8 teaspoon pepper

Mix lime juice, oil and red pepper in large glass or plastic bowl. Cut each chicken wing at joints to make 3 pieces; discard tip. Cut off and discard excess skin. Place wings in oil mixture; stir to coat. Cover and refrigerate at least 3 hours but no longer than 24 hours, stirring occasionally; drain.

Heat oven to 425°. Melt margarine in rectangular pan, 13×9×2 inches, in oven. Shake remaining ingredients in plastic bag, or mix in bowl. Shake wings in cornmeal mixture to coat; place in pan.

Bake uncovered 20 minutes; turn. Bake 20 to 25 minutes longer or until juice is no longer pink when centers of thickest pieces are cut.

1 Serving: Calories 110 (Calories from Fat 70); Fat 8g (Saturated 2g); Cholesterol 15 mg; Sodium 80 mg; Carbohydrate 4g (Dietary Fiber 0g); Protein 5g

Bell Pepper Nachos

6 SERVINGS

1/2 green bell pepper, seeded and cut into 6 strips

1/2 red bell pepper, seeded and cut into 6 strips

1/2 yellow bell pepper, seeded and cut into 6 strips

3/4 cup shredded Monterey Jack cheese (3 ounces)

2 tablespoons chopped ripe olives

1/4 teaspoon crushed red pepper

Line broilerproof pan, 9×1 1/4 inches, or round pan, 9×2 inches with aluminum foil. Cut bell pepper strips crosswise in half. Arrange close together in pan. Sprinkle with cheese, olives and red pepper.

Set oven control to broil. Broil peppers with tops 3 to 4 inches from heat about 3 minutes or until cheese is melted.

1 Serving: Calories 65 (Calories from Fat 45); Fat 5g (Saturated 3g); Cholesterol 15 mg; Sodium 110 mg; Carbohydrate 2g (Dietary Fiber 0g); Protein 3g

Bell Pepper Nachos

Quesadillas

6 SERVINGS

2 cups shredded Colby or Cheddar cheese (8 ounces)

6 flour tortillas (8 or 10 inches in diameter)

1 small tomato, chopped (1/2 cup)

1/4 cup chopped green onions (3 medium)

2 tablespoons canned chopped green chilies

Chopped fresh cilantro or parsley

Heat oven to 350°. Sprinkle 1/3 cup of the cheese evenly over half of each tortilla. Top cheese with remaining ingredients. Fold tortilla over filling. Place on ungreased cookie sheet.

Bake about 5 minutes or just until cheese is melted. Serve quesadillas whole, or cut each into 3 wedges, beginning cuts from center of folded sides.

1 Serving: Calories 290 (Calories from Fat 145); Fat 16g (Saturated 8g); Cholesterol 40 mg; Sodium 470 mg; Carbohydrate 25g (Dietary Fiber 1g); Protein 13g

Super Chicken Nachos

6 SERVINGS

1 package (6 ounces) tortilla chips

1/2 cup chopped ripe avocado

1/2 teaspoon ground cumin

1 can (11 ounces) tomatillos, drained

1 cup shredded cooked chicken

1 cup shredded Monterey Jack cheese (4 ounces)

Salsa and sour cream, if desired

Heat oven to 400°. Line cookie sheet with aluminum foil. Place tortilla chips on cookie sheet. Mix avocado, cumin and tomatillos; spoon over chips. Top with chicken and cheese.

Bake 3 to 5 minutes or until cheese is melted. Serve with salsa and sour cream.

1 Serving: Calories 265 (Calories from Fat 135); Fat 15g (Saturated 5g); Cholesterol 40 mg; Sodium 440 mg; Carbohydrate 21g (Dietary Fiber 2g); Protein 14g

Nifty Nachos

5 SERVINGS

Some like it hot! For a spicy variation of this popular snack, substitute 6 jalapeño chilies, seeded and each cut into 6 strips, or 1/4 cup canned chopped green chilies for the salsa.

30 round tortilla chips

1/4 cup salsa

1 1/4 cups shredded Monterey Jack or Cheddar cheese (5 ounces)

Heat oven to 400°. Line cookie sheet with aluminum foil. Place tortilla chips on cookie sheet. Top with salsa. Sprinkle with cheese.

Bake 3 to 5 minutes or until cheese is melted.

1 Serving: Calories 155 (Calories from Fat 100); Fat 11g (Saturated 6g); Cholesterol 25 mg; Sodium 350 mg; Carbohydrate 8g (Dietary Fiber 1g); Protein 7g

Potato Skins Olé

8 SERVINGS (2 SHELLS EACH)

In this Tex-Mex version of a popular appetizer, the potato skins are baked, not fried.

4 large potatoes (about 2 pounds), baked

2 tablespoons margarine or butter, melted

1 cup shredded Colby-Monterey Jack cheese (4 ounces)

1/2 cup sour cream

1/2 cup sliced green onions (5 medium)

1/4 cup salsa

Let potatoes stand until cool enough to handle. Cut potatoes lengthwise into fourths; carefully scoop out pulp, leaving 1/4-inch shells. Save potato pulp for another use.

Set oven control to broil. Place potato shells, skin sides down, in broiler pan. Brush potato flesh with margarine. Broil 4 to 5 inches from heat 8 to 10 minutes or until crisp and brown.

Sprinkle cheese over potato shells. Broil about 30 seconds or until cheese is melted. Mix sour cream and onions; spoon onto potatoes. Top with salsa.

1 Serving: Calories 175 (Calories from Fat 90); Fat 10g (Saturated 5g); Cholesterol 25 mg; Sodium 180 mg; Carbohydrate 17g (Dietary Fiber 1g); Protein 5g

Jalapeño Surprise

16 SQUARES

A layer of eggs hides a delicious mix of chilies and cheese. To make this dish into tostadas, cut the entire recipe into 4 squares and place each on a heated tostada shell. Garnish with lettuce and tomatoes.

1/4 cup canned diced jalapeño chilies, drained

1 cup shredded Cheddar cheese (4 ounces)

6 eggs, beaten

1/4 teaspoon chili powder

Heat oven to 350°. Spray square pan, $8 \times 8 \times 2$ inches, with nonstick cooking spray. Spread chilies in bottom of pan. Sprinkle with cheese. Pour eggs over chilies and cheese. Sprinkle with chili powder.

Bake uncovered about 20 minutes or until eggs are set. Let stand 5 minutes. Cut into 2-inch squares.

1 Serving: Calories 50 (Calories from Fat 35); Fat 4g (Saturated 2g); Cholesterol 85 mg; Sodium 90 mg; Carbohydrate 0g (Dietary Fiber 0g); Protein 4g

Chîle con Queso

ABOUT 1 1/4 CUPS DIP

1 cup shredded Cheddar or Monterey Jack cheese (4 ounces)

1/4 cup half-and-half

2 tablespoons finely chopped onion

2 teaspoons ground cumin

1/2 teaspoon salt

1 can (4 ounces) chopped green chilies, drained

Tortilla chips, if desired

Place all ingredients except tortilla chips in 1-quart saucepan. Heat over low heat, stirring constantly, until cheese is melted. Serve with tortilla chips.

1 Serving: Calories 25 (Calories from Fat 20); Fat 2g (Saturated 1g); Cholesterol 5 mg; Sodium 150 mg; Carbohydrate 1g (Dietary Fiber 0g); Protein 1g

Mexican Appetîzer Ring

12 WEDGES

Here's a picture-perfect "pizza" with a Mexican accent to cut into wedges and serve with forks.

1 refrigerated pie crust (from 15-ounce package)

1 can (16 ounces) refried beans

1 can (6 ounces) frozen guacamole, thawed

1 package (3 ounces) cream cheese, softened

2 tablespoons salsa

3 cherry tomatoes, sliced

3 ripe olives, sliced

2 green onions, sliced

Heat oven to 450°. Place pie crust on 12-inch pizza pan or cookie sheet. Flute edge; prick crust with fork. Bake 8 to 10 minutes or until golden brown; cool completely.

Spread beans on crust to within 1/2 inch of edge. Spoon guacamole in a circle on beans about 1 1/2 inches from edge of crust; gently spread guacamole into 2-inch ring. Mix cream cheese and salsa; spoon into middle of guacamole ring. Garnish ring with tomatoes, olives and onions. Cover and refrigerate until serving time. Cut into wedges.

1 Serving: Calories 170 (Calories from Fat 100); Fat 11g (Saturated 5g); Cholesterol 10 mg; Sodium 340 mg; Carbohydrate 17g (Dietary Fiber 3g); Protein 4g

Mexîcan Pinwheels

ABOUT 30 SLICES

1/2 cup sour cream

1/2 cup finely shredded Cheddar cheese (2 ounces)

1/4 cup finely chopped red bell pepper

2 tablespoons finely chopped ripe olives

2 tablespoons canned chopped green chilies

1 tablespoon chopped fresh parsley

1 package (3 ounces) cream cheese, softened

3 flour tortillas (8 or 10 inches in diameter)

Mix all ingredients except tortillas. Spread cheese mixture evenly over tortillas; roll up tortillas. Wrap tortilla rolls individually in plastic wrap. Refrigerate up to 24 hours. Cut into 1-inch slices.

1 Serving: Calories 45 (Calories from Fat 25); Fat 3g (Saturated 2g); Cholesterol 10 mg; Sodium 55 mg; Carbohydrate 3g (Dietary Fiber 0g); Protein 1g

Snappy Stuffed Pepper

8 SERVINGS

1 large bell pepper

2/3 cup shredded Cheddar cheese

1/2 cup whole kernel corn

2 packages (3 ounces each) cream cheese, softened

3 tablespoons milk

2 green onions, sliced

1 1/2 teaspoons chili powder

Chili powder

Crackers or raw vegetables, if desired

Cut 1/2-inch slice from top of bell pepper and remove stem; chop remaining pepper top and set aside. Remove seeds and membrane from pepper. If necessary, cut thin layer from bottom of pepper so it rests flat on serving plate.

Mix chopped pepper, the Cheddar cheese, corn, cream cheese, milk, onions and 1 1/2 teaspoons chili powder. Fill pepper with cheese mixture. Sprinkle with chili powder. Cover and refrigerate until serving time. Serve with crackers.

1 Serving: Calories 125 (Calories from Fat 100); Fat 11g (Saturated 7g); Cholesterol 35 mg; Sodium 170 mg; Carbohydrate 4g (Dietary Fiber 1g); Protein 4g

Cheese Chile

48 SERVINGS

1 cup shredded Cheddar cheese (4 ounces)

1 cup shredded Colby cheese (4 ounces)

1 teaspoon chili powder

Paprika

Place cheeses and chili powder in food processor. Cover and process about 1 minute or until smooth. Roll mixture into shape of chile. Sprinkle with paprika. Cover and refrigerate until serving time.

Do-Ahead Tip: Cover and refrigerate Cheese Chile up to 1 week.

1 Serving: Calories 20 (Calories from Fat 20); Fat 2g (Saturated 1g); Cholesterol 5 mg; Sodium 30 mg; Carbohydrate 0g (Dietary Fiber 0g); Protein 1g

Marinated Jicama Appetizer

ABOUT 3 1/2 DOZEN APPETIZERS

1 jicama (about 2 pounds)

1/4 cup lemon or lime juice

1 teaspoon salt

1 teaspoon chili powder

Peel jicama; cut into fourths. Cut each fourth into 1/4-inch slices. Arrange slices on serving plate. Drizzle with lemon juice. Sprinkle with salt and chili powder. Cover and refrigerate at least 2 hours to blend flavors.

1 Serving: Calories 10 (Calories from Fat 0); Fat 0g (Saturated 0g); Cholesterol 0 mg; Sodium 55 mg; Carbohydrate 2g (Dietary Fiber 0g); Protein 0g

Following pages: Assorted chilies (clockwise from top of photograph): Jalapeño (green and red, in spoon), poblano, ancho, pasilla, serrano, cascabel, guajillo, jalapeño (red), serrano (yellow and orange), jalapeño (green and red), Anaheim (green and red, in bag), serrano and chipotle.

Chîle Prîmer

Chilies are native to the Americas. They have been known in North America for some time but are said to have traveled north by a circuitous route; apparently they found their way from Mexico to Europe with Christopher Columbus, then to the East and finally back to North America.

New strains of chilies are developed frequently, bred for hardiness, sweetness and hotness for example. But chilies are full of surprises; two chilies picked from the same plant may vary widely in hotness. To quench the fire of a too-spicy mouthful, don't reach for water. Water will only spread the capsaicin (the compound that our tongues register as "hot") around. Instead, take a large mouthful of something starchy such as corn chips, beans, bread or rice.

Sometimes finding fresh chilies is difficult. This probably isn't a question of availability, but because they are quite perishable. Canned and dried chilies are usually found in most large supermarkets.

Types of Chilies

Anaheim chilies (California green chilies) are slim, between 5 and 8 inches long, and of various light shades of green. These mildly hot chilies are sometimes twisted in appearance. They are occasionally stuffed, but their flesh is thin and more fragile than that of poblano chilies. The Anaheims cultivated in New Mexico—where the name is chile verde—are reportedly hotter. A ripe, red Anaheim is sometimes known as a Colorado chile. Anaheim chilies are sometimes dried and tied in wreathes (*ristras*) and ground and blended in commercial chili powder mixtures. They may be purchased in cans as "mild green chilies." These chilies were named after the town that, at the turn of the century, was the site of a chile cannery.

Ancho refers to a ripened, dried poblano chile.

Cascabel chilies, true ones, are scarce in most parts of the United States. Sometimes dried Anaheim chilies are labeled "cascabel," but they are very different from authentic cascabels. Fresh cascabels are hot and have a distinctive flavor. They are round, and about 1 1/2 inches in diameter. When dried, the cascabel chile has a nutlike flavor.

Cayenne chilies are thin, tapered and 3 to 7 inches long. Dark green (unripe) or bright red (ripe), the cayenne is very hot and is used in Asian cuisine as well as Mexican. The red ones are dried and ground to make ground red pepper, also known as cayenne pepper. This product adds mainly heat and just a little chile flavor.

Chili powder is a mixture of ground, dried red chilies blended with other spices and herbs. It is said to have been invented by Willie Gebhardt, a Texan, in 1892. Most brands contain cumin and oregano and may include paprika, coriander and salt. Chili powder should not be confused with ground red chilies (see below).

Chipotle chilies are smoked, dried jalapeños with a very wrinkled appearance. Fresh jalapeños are vibrant green but they turn brown when smoked. Chipotles can be purchased dry or canned in adobo sauce (a seasoned, tomato-based sauce). The canned variety is especially convenient as it saves having to soak and soften them.

Crushed red pepper (red pepper flakes) are flaked, dried ripe red chilies. Most crushed red pepper mixtures are quite hot.

Ground red chilies are pure chile powder made from finely ground, dried red chilies and contain no other ingredients.

Guajillo chilies (mirasol chilies) are dried and have a hot, fruity flavor. Guajillos are orange-red, skinny and about 2 to 3 inches long. When fresh, the chile is referred to as a mirasol chile.

Jalapeño chilies range from hot to very hot. They are dark green, fat and about 2 to 3 inches long with a rounded tip. Watch out for the little ones, which are hottest. When ripe, jalapeños turn bright red. Jalapeños can be used fresh or pickled.

Pasilla chilies are hot and brown (almost black when dried, which is how they are commonly found). They have an earthy flavor.

Poblano is the chile most frequently used for chiles rellenos. It is dark green and ranges from mild to hot. Shaped like a long, tapered bell pepper, the poblano is shaped nicely for stuffing.

Serrano chilies are extremely hot and bright to dark green, developing to brilliant red when ripe. Serranos are shorter and thinner than the jalapeño.

(Continued on next page)

Chile Safety

The flesh, ribs and seeds of chilies are rich in irritating, burning oils called capsaicins (pronounced "cap-say-sins"), with the highest capsaicin concentration being in the ribs. Because the seeds are so close to the ribs, they are usually hot as well. You may want to wear plastic gloves or place your hands in plastic sandwich bags when cutting up chilies. When processing chilies in a blender or food processor, turn your face away because the fumes are burning. When preparing chilies, always wash hands and utensils in soapy water. Be especially careful not to rub your face—eyes in particular—until the oils have been thoroughly washed away.

Roasting Chilies

Recipes often call for chilies or bell peppers to be roasted. This enhances the flavor, as toasting brings out the flavor of nuts, and makes them easy to peel. Roasted chilies or peppers may be frozen before peeling, a convenience if you roast a big batch at once; wrap them airtight in plastic wrap.

Broiler method: Set oven control to broil. Remove stem; cut chilies or bell peppers into halves or quarters. Remove ribs and seeds. Arrange chilies or bell peppers, skin sides up, on broiler rack in broiler pan or cookie sheet 5 to 6 inches from the heat. Broil until the skin is blistered and evenly browned (some areas may blacken). Remove chilies or bell peppers and place in a paper bag; close tightly and allow chilies to steam for 20 minutes to loosen skin, then peel.

Larger chilies or bell peppers will roast in about 5 to 7 minutes; small chilies, in about 5 minutes.

Gas stove-top method: Spear a *whole* chile or bell pepper on a long-handled metal fork with a heatproof handle and hold it about 5 inches from the flame. Turn the chile or bell pepper so that it roasts evenly. Roast until the skin is blistered and evenly browned (some areas may blacken). Remove chilies or bell peppers and place in a paper bag; close tightly and allow chilies to steam for 20 minutes to loosen skin, then peel. Cut open and remove ribs and seeds. Larger chilies or bell peppers will roast in about 5 to 7 minutes; small chilies, in about 2 to 3 minutes. The disadvantage of this method is that you can't roast a number of chilies at once.

Corn and Walnut Dip

ABOUT 2 CUPS DIP

1 package (8 ounces) cream cheese, softened

1/4 cup milk

2 tablespoons lime juice

1 1/2 teaspoons chili powder

1 1/2 teaspoons ground cumin

1/4 teaspoon salt

Dash of pepper

1/2 cup frozen whole kernel corn, thawed

1/2 cup chopped walnuts, toasted
    (page 119)

2 tablespoons chopped onion

Tortilla chips, if desired

Beat cream cheese, milk, lime juice, chili powder, cumin, salt and pepper in medium bowl with electric mixer on medium speed until smooth. Stir in corn, walnuts and onion. Serve with tortilla chips.

1 Serving: Calories 35 (Calories from Fat 25); Fat 3g (Saturated 2g); Cholesterol 10 mg; Sodium 40 mg; Carbohydrate 1g (Dietary Fiber 0g); Protein 1g

Black-Eyed Peas Mexicana

ABOUT 3 CUPS RELISH

This colorful vegetable combination is often called "Texas Caviar" and can be served as an appetizer with chips or as a salad on lettuce leaves.

1 can (15 to 16 ounces) black-eyed peas,
    rinsed and drained

1 medium tomato, chopped (3/4 cup)

1 small green bell pepper, chopped (1/2 cup)

4 green onions, thinly sliced

1 clove garlic, finely chopped

1/3 cup salsa

2 tablespoons chopped fresh cilantro

Mix all ingredients in glass or plastic bowl. Cover and refrigerate at least 2 hours to blend flavors.

1 Serving: Calories 20 (Calories from Fat 0); Fat 0g (Saturated 0g); Cholesterol 0 mg; Sodium 120 mg; Carbohydrate 8g (Dietary Fiber 4g); Protein 4g

Quick Guacamole

ABOUT 2 CUPS DIP

2 large ripe avocados, mashed

1/3 cup thick-and-chunky salsa

1 tablespoon lime juice

Tortilla chips, if desired

Mix avocados, salsa and lime juice in glass or plastic bowl. Serve with tortilla chips.

1 Serving: Calories 20 (Calories from Fat 20); Fat 2g (Saturated 0g); Cholesterol 0 mg; Sodium 20 mg; Carbohydrate 1g (Dietary Fiber 0g); Protein 0g

---

SALSAS

Salsas are sassy, chunky, spicy, mild, sweet, tart, savory, salty and more! The idea of salsa isn't really new. Salsas are a version of a condiment, and condiments have been around for a very long time. Almost every country has an array of condiments that are used regularly to enliven foods. Of course, the common Mexican salsa, with its combination of tomatoes, chilies or peppers and onion, is very familiar to us. But the world is filled with many delicious "salsas," such as harissa, the fiery hot chile pepper-based sauce of Tunisia, or raita, the cool and creamy yogurt sauce from India. You may recall flavor-packed favorites from your own past, such as piccalilli, chow-chow, chutney and a wide variety of relishes. And where would hamburgers and hot dogs be without ketchup and mustard?

Contemporary salsas have gained tremendous popularity. Different combinations of vegetables, fruits, peppers, beans and nuts blended with herbs, spices, vinegars, and lemon and lime juices perk up any plain recipe. The majority of these salsas are uncooked and generally low in calories and fat, offering vibrant flavors and colors with plenty of interesting textures. You'll find our tempting salsa recipes on pages 21 to 24.

Salsa Serving Ideas

- Spoon over any cooked meat, poultry or seafood. Salsas are especially tasty with grilled foods.

- Serve with tortilla chips, assorted crackers or pita bread.

- Serve tomato-based salsa with cooked eggs or quiche.

- Serve on baked potatoes or other cooked vegetables.

- Toss with cooked rice or pasta.

- Use as a sandwich filling or a sandwich topping.

- Serve with enchiladas, burritos or tacos.

- Use as a pizza topping.

- Use as a garnish for soup or chili.

- Serve as a side dish.

Fresh Tomato Salsa

ABOUT 3 1/2 CUPS SALSA

Fully ripe, juicy red tomatoes and freshly squeezed lime juice give the best flavor to this salsa.

3 medium tomatoes, seeded and chopped
    (2 1/4 cups)

1 small green bell pepper, chopped (1/2 cup)

3 cloves garlic, finely chopped

1/2 cup sliced green onions (5 medium)

2 tablespoons chopped fresh cilantro or
    parsley

1 tablespoon finely chopped jalapeño chilies

2 to 3 tablespoons lime juice

1/4 teaspoon salt

Mix all ingredients in glass or plastic bowl. Cover and refrigerate at least 1 hour to blend flavors.

1 Serving: Calories 20 (Calories from Fat 0); Fat 0g (Saturated 0g); Cholesterol 0 mg; Sodium 40 mg; Carbohydrate 4g (Dietary Fiber 0g); Protein 0g

Mexican Flag Salsa

ABOUT 3 CUPS SALSA

2 tablespoons chopped fresh parsley

3 tablespoons lime juice

1 tablespoon vegetable oil

2 teaspoons sugar

3/4 teaspoon crushed red pepper

1/4 teaspoon salt

2 cloves garlic, finely chopped

1 1/2 cups diced peeled jicama

1/2 cup diced cucumber

1 small red bell pepper, diced (1/2 cup)

1 small green bell pepper, diced (1/2 cup)

1/3 cup sliced green onions (4 medium)

1/2 cup dry-roasted peanuts, coarsely
    chopped

Mix parsley, lime juice, oil, sugar, red pepper, salt and garlic in medium glass or plastic bowl. Add jicama, cucumber, bell peppers and onions; toss. Cover and refrigerate at least 2 hours to blend flavors. Stir in peanuts just before serving.

1 Serving: Calories 60 (Calories from Fat 40); Fat 4g (Saturated 0g); Cholesterol 0 mg; Sodium 120 mg; Carbohydrate 4g (Dietary Fiber 0g); Protein 0g

Jicama-Cucumber Salsa

ABOUT 3 CUPS SALSA

2 cups chopped peeled jicama (12 ounces)

1 tablespoon chopped fresh cilantro or parsley

1 tablespoon lime juice

1/2 teaspoon chili powder

1/4 teaspoon salt

1 medium cucumber, peeled and chopped (1 cup)

1 medium orange, peeled and chopped (3/4 cup)

Mix all ingredients in glass or plastic bowl. Cover and refrigerate at least 2 hours to blend flavors.

1 Serving: Calories 20 (Calories from Fat 0); Fat 0g (Saturated 0g); Cholesterol 0 mg; Sodium 10 mg; Carbohydrate 4g (Dietary Fiber 0g); Protein 0g

Melon-Jicama Salsa

ABOUT 2 1/2 CUPS SALSA

1 cup chopped cantaloupe

1 cup chopped honeydew melon

1/2 cup chopped peeled jicama

2 tablespoons sliced green onions

2 tablespoons chopped fresh cilantro or parsley

1 tablespoon finely chopped gingerroot

2 tablespoons lime juice

1 jalapeño chile, seeded and finely chopped

Mix all ingredients in glass or plastic bowl. Cover and refrigerate at least 1 hour to blend flavors.

1 Serving: Calories 20 (Calories from Fat 0); Fat 0g (Saturated 0g); Cholesterol 0 mg; Sodium 0 mg; Carbohydrate 4g (Dietary Fiber 0g); Protein 0g

Pineapple Salsa

ABOUT 2 1/2 CUPS SALSA

2 cups 1/2-inch pieces pineapple (1/2 medium)

1/4 cup finely chopped red onion

2 tablespoons chopped fresh cilantro or parsley

2 tablespoons lime juice

1 small red bell pepper, chopped (1/2 cup)

1 small red chile, seeded and finely chopped

Mix all ingredients in glass or plastic bowl. Cover and refrigerate at least 1 hour to blend flavors.

1 Serving: Calories 20 (Calories from Fat 0); Fat 0g (Saturated 0g); Cholesterol 0 mg; Sodium 0 mg; Carbohydrate 4g (Dietary Fiber 0g); Protein 0g

Mexican Flag Salsa (page 21); Pineapple Salsa; Corn-Olive Salsa (page 24)

Corn-Olive Salsa

ABOUT 2 1/3 CUPS SALSA

1 can (16 ounces) whole kernel corn, drained

1 can (4 ounces) chopped green chilies, drained

1 can (2 1/4 ounces) sliced ripe olives, drained

1 jalapeño chile, seeded and finely chopped

2 tablespoons white wine vinegar

1 tablespoon vegetable oil

1/4 teaspoon salt

Mix all ingredients in glass or plastic bowl. Cover and refrigerate at least 1 hour to blend flavors.

1 Serving: Calories 60 (Calories from Fat 40); Fat 4g (Saturated 0g); Cholesterol 0 mg; Sodium 380 mg; Carbohydrate 8g (Dietary Fiber 0g); Protein 0g

Radish and Cilantro Relish

ABOUT 2 1/2 CUPS RELISH

24 medium radishes, thinly sliced (2 cups)

1 medium onion, chopped (1/2 cup)

2 tablespoons chopped fresh cilantro or parsley

3 tablespoons orange juice

2 tablespoons lime juice

2 tablespoons vegetable oil

1/4 teaspoon salt

1/8 teaspoon freshly ground pepper

Mix all ingredients in glass or plastic bowl. Cover and refrigerate at least 1 hour to blend flavors.

1 Serving: Calories 40 (Calories from Fat 25); Fat 3g (Saturated 1g); Cholesterol 0 mg; Sodium 60 mg; Carbohydrate 3g (Dietary Fiber 0g); Protein 0g

Black Bean Relish

ABOUT 2 1/2 CUPS RELISH

1 can (15 ounces) black beans, rinsed and drained

1 large tomato, finely chopped (1 cup)

1 small red bell pepper, chopped (1/2 cup)

1 serrano or jalapeño chile, seeded and finely chopped

1/4 cup finely chopped red onion

2 tablespoons white wine vinegar

1 tablespoon vegetable oil

1/4 teaspoon salt

Mix all ingredients in glass or plastic bowl. Cover and refrigerate at least 1 hour to blend flavors.

1 Serving: Calories 60 (Calories from Fat 0); Fat 0g (Saturated 0g); Cholesterol 0 mg; Sodium 140 mg; Carbohydrate 12g (Dietary Fiber 0g); Protein 4g

Tomatillo Sauce

ABOUT **1 1/4** CUPS SAUCE

8 ounces tomatillos or small green tomatoes, cut in half

2 canned serrano chilies, rinsed and seeded, or 1 fresh serrano chile, seeded

1/4 cup chopped red onion

1/4 cup chopped fresh cilantro or parsley

1/4 teaspoon salt

Place all ingredients in food processor or blender. Cover and process until well blended.

1 Serving: Calories 20 (Calories from Fat 0); Fat 0g (Saturated 0g); Cholesterol 0 mg; Sodium 300 mg; Carbohydrate 4g (Dietary Fiber 0g); Protein 0g

Cilantro Pesto

ABOUT **1 1/4** CUPS PESTO

1 1/2 cups firmly packed fresh cilantro

1/2 cup firmly packed fresh parsley

1/2 cup grated Parmesan cheese

1/2 cup vegetable oil

1/4 teaspoon salt

3 cloves garlic

1/4 cup pine nuts

Place all ingredients in food processor or blender. Cover and process until well blended.

1 Serving: Calories 70 (Calories from Fat 65); Fat 7g (Saturated 1g); Cholesterol 0 mg; Sodium 65 mg; Carbohydrate 1g (Dietary Fiber 0g); Protein 1g

Chipotle Mayonnaise

ABOUT **1** CUP MAYONNAISE

2 canned chipotle chilies in adobo sauce, finely chopped

1/2 cup mayonnaise or salad dressing

1/2 cup sour cream

1/8 teaspoon dried oregano leaves, if desired

Mix all ingredients. Cover and refrigerate at least 1 hour to blend flavors.

1 Serving: Calories 65 (Calories from Fat 65); Fat 7g (Saturated 2g); Cholesterol 10 mg; Sodium 110 mg; Carbohydrate 1g (Dietary Fiber 0g); Protein 0g

2

Tortîllas

Beef Burritos (page 28)

Beef Burritos

8 SERVINGS

A burrito is a flour tortilla wrapped envelope-style around a filling and baked.

- **8 flour tortillas (8 or 10 inches in diameter)**
- **1 can (16 ounces) refried beans**
- **2 cups shredded cooked beef**
- **2 cups shredded lettuce**
- **1 large tomato, chopped (1 cup)**
- **1 cup shredded Cheddar or Monterey Jack cheese (4 ounces)**

Spread each tortilla with about 2 tablespoons of the beans. Place 1/4 cup of the beef on center of each tortilla. Top with lettuce, tomato and cheese.

Fold one end of tortilla up about 1 inch over filling; fold right and left sides over folded end, overlapping. Fold remaining end down. Place seam side down on serving platter or plate. Serve with salsa, if desired.

1 Serving: Calories 235 (Calories from Fat 125); Fat 14g (Saturated 6g); Cholesterol 45 mg; Sodium 560 mg; Carbohydrate 36g (Dietary Fiber 4g); Protein 20g

Picnic Burritos

6 SERVINGS

- **1/2 cup mayonnaise or salad dressing**
- **2 teaspoons taco seasoning mix (from 1 1/4-ounce envelope)**
- **6 flour tortillas (8 or 10 inches in diameter)**
- **1/2 cup shredded Cheddar cheese (2 ounces)**
- **1/2 pound thinly sliced cooked turkey**
- **1 large tomato, thinly sliced**
- **Leaf lettuce**

Mix mayonnaise and seasoning mix in a bowl; spread on each tortilla. Layer each tortilla with remaining ingredients, leaving a 2-inch rim on one side of tortilla.

Beginning at side layered with ingredients, roll up each tortilla. To serve immediately, cut in half. Or securely wrap uncut burritos with plastic wrap and refrigerate up to 2 hours; cut in half.

1 Serving: Calories 360 (Calories from Fat 200); Fat 22g (Saturated 5g); Cholesterol 35 mg; Sodium 870 mg; Carbohydrate 28g (Dietary Fiber 1g); Protein 13g

Folding Up a Burrito

1. Fold up 1 end of tortilla about 1 inch over beef mixture

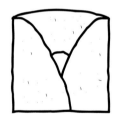

2. Fold right and left sides over folded end, overlapping.

3. Fold down remaining end.

Chicken Burritos

6 SERVINGS

Jicama-Cucumber Salsa (page 22)
1 tablespoon vegetable oil
1 large onion, chopped (1 cup)
1 clove garlic, finely chopped
2 cups chopped cooked chicken or turkey
2/3 cup chicken broth
1 1/4 teaspoons chili powder
1/4 teaspoon salt
1/4 teaspoon pepper
6 flour tortillas (8 or 10 inches in diameter)
1 tablespoon margarine or butter, softened

Prepare Jicama-Cucumber Salsa; reserve. Heat oil in 10-inch skillet over medium-high heat. Cook onion and garlic in oil about 3 minutes, stirring occasionally, until onion is crisp-tender. Stir in chicken, broth, chili powder, salt and pepper; reduce heat. Cook about 10 minutes or until liquid is absorbed.

Heat oven to 500°. Spoon about 1/3 cup of the chicken mixture onto center of each tortilla. Fold one end of tortilla up about 1 inch over mixture; fold right and left sides over folded end, overlapping. Fold remaining end down. Place seam side down on ungreased cookie sheet. Brush with margarine.

Bake 8 to 10 minutes or until tortillas begin to brown and filling is hot. Serve with salsa.

1 Serving: Calories 260 (Calories from Fat 90); Fat 10g (Saturated 3g); Cholesterol 40 mg; Sodium 440 mg; Carbohydrate 27g (Dietary Fiber 2g); Protein 18g

Pepita Vegetable Burritos

6 SERVINGS

2 tablespoons vegetable oil
1 cup chopped broccoli
1 medium onion, finely chopped (1/2 cup)
2 cloves garlic, finely chopped
1 cup 2 × 1/4-inch strips yellow squash
1 cup 2 × 1/4-inch strips zucchini
1/2 cup finely chopped red bell pepper
1/4 cup shelled pumpkin seeds, toasted (page 120)
1 tablespoon lemon juice
1 teaspoon chili powder
1/4 teaspoon salt
1/4 teaspoon ground cumin
6 flour tortillas (8 or 10 inches in diameter), warmed (page 42)

Heat oil in 10-inch skillet over medium-high heat. Cook broccoli, onion and garlic in oil, stirring frequently, until tender. Stir in remaining ingredients except tortillas. Cook about 2 minutes, stirring occasionally, until squash is crisp-tender; keep warm.

Spoon about 1/2 cup of the vegetable mixture onto center of each tortilla. Fold one end of tortilla up about 1 inch over mixture; fold right and left sides over folded end, overlapping. Fold remaining end down. Serve with desired toppings.

1 Serving: Calories 220 (Calories from Fat 90); Fat 10g (Saturated 2g); Cholesterol 0 mg; Sodium 330 mg; Carbohydrate 29g (Dietary Fiber 3g); Protein 7g

Red Enchiladas with Cheese

6 SERVINGS

2 tablespoons vegetable oil

1 large onion, finely chopped (1 cup)

2 cloves garlic, finely chopped

1 1/2 cups chicken broth

8 medium tomatoes, seeded and chopped (6 cups)

1 tablespoon chili powder

1 teaspoon salt

1 teaspoon ground cumin

1 teaspoon dried oregano leaves

1/8 teaspoon pepper

12 corn or flour tortillas (6 or 8 inches in diameter)

3 cups shredded Cheddar or Monterey Jack cheese (12 ounces)

Sour cream

Heat oil in 12-inch skillet over medium-high heat. Cook onion and garlic in oil, stirring occasionally, until onion is tender. Stir in broth, tomatoes, chili powder, salt, cumin, oregano and pepper. Heat to boiling; reduce heat. Simmer uncovered 1 hour, stirring occasionally.

Heat oven to 350°. Dip each tortilla into sauce to coat both sides. Spoon 2 tablespoons of the cheese down center of each tortilla. Roll up tortilla; place seam side down in ungreased rectangular baking dish, $13 \times 9 \times 2$ inches. Pour remaining sauce over tortillas. Sprinkle with remaining cheese.

Bake uncovered 15 to 20 minutes or until cheese is melted. Serve with sour cream.

1 Serving: Calories 465 (Calories from Fat 260); Fat 29g (Saturated 15g); Cholesterol 70 mg; Sodium 1020 mg; Carbohydrate 36g (Dietary Fiber 5g); Protein 20g

Green Enchiladas

5 SERVINGS

Tomatillo Sauce (page 25) or 1 1/4 cups green salsa (salsa verde)

1 cup sour cream

10 corn or flour tortillas (6 or 8 inches in diameter), warmed (page 42)

3 cups shredded cooked chicken

1 cup shredded Monterey Jack cheese (4 ounces)

Sour cream

Prepare Tomatillo Sauce; stir in 1 cup sour cream.

Heat oven to 350°. Dip each tortilla into sauce to coat both sides. Spoon 1/4 cup of the chicken down center of each tortilla. Roll up tortilla; place seam side down in ungreased rectangular baking dish, $13 \times 9 \times 2$ inches. Pour remaining sauce over tortillas. Sprinkle with cheese.

Bake uncovered about 15 minutes or until cheese is melted. Serve with sour cream.

1 Serving: Calories 480 (Calories from Fat 230); Fat 26g (Saturated 14g); Cholesterol 135 mg; Sodium 720 mg; Carbohydrate 30g (Dietary Fiber 4g); Protein 35g

Baked Chimichangas

4 SERVINGS

1 pound ground beef

1 small onion, finely chopped (1/4 cup)

1 clove garlic, finely chopped

1/4 cup slivered almonds

1/4 cup raisins

1 tablespoon red wine vinegar

1 teaspoon chili powder

1/2 teaspoon salt

1/4 teaspoon ground cinnamon

1/8 teaspoon ground cloves

1 medium tomato, seeded and chopped
   (3/4 cup)

1 can (4 ounces) chopped green chilies,
   drained

8 flour tortillas (8 or 10 inches in diameter),
   warmed (page 42)

2 tablespoons margarine or butter, softened

Guacamole, salsa or sour cream, if desired

Cook beef, onion and garlic in 10-inch skillet over medium-high heat, stirring occasionally, until beef is brown; drain. Stir in remaining ingredients except tortillas, margarine and guacamole. Heat to boiling; reduce heat. Simmer uncovered 20 minutes, stirring occasionally.

Heat oven to 500°. Spoon about 1/2 cup of the beef mixture onto center of each tortilla. Fold one end of tortilla up about 1 inch over beef mixture; fold right and left sides over folded end, overlapping. Fold remaining end down. Brush each chimichanga with margarine.

Place seam sides down in ungreased jelly roll pan, 15 1/2 × 10 1/2 × 1 inch. Bake 8 to 10 minutes or until tortillas begin to brown and filling is hot. Serve with guacamole.

Fried Chimichangas: Omit margarine or butter. Heat oil (about 1 inch) to 365°. Fry 2 or 3 chimichangas at a time in oil 3 to 4 minutes, turning once, until golden brown. Keep warm in 300° oven.

1 Serving: Calories 635 (Calories from Fat 290); Fat 32g (Saturated 9g); Cholesterol 65 mg; Sodium 1010 mg; Carbohydrate 61g (Dietary Fiber 4g); Protein 30g

Taco Joes

10 SERVINGS

1 pound ground beef

1 medium stalk celery, chopped (1/2 cup)

1 medium onion, chopped (1/2 cup)

1 jar (16 ounces) salsa (about 2 cups)

1 can (about 15 ounces) whole kernel corn,
   drained

10 taco shells

Shredded lettuce, if desired

Cook beef in 10-inch skillet over medium-high heat, stirring occasionally, until brown; drain. Stir in celery, onion, salsa and corn. Heat to boiling, stirring constantly; reduce heat to low. Simmer uncovered 5 minutes, stirring occasionally.

Heat taco shells as directed on package. Spoon beef mixture into taco shells. Top with lettuce.

1 Serving: Calories 200 (Calories from Fat 90); Fat 10g (Saturated 3g); Cholesterol 25 mg; Sodium 460 mg; Carbohydrate 19g (Dietary Fiber 3g); Protein 11g

Grilled Pork Tacos

4 SERVINGS

Pineapple Salsa (page 22)

1 tablespoon margarine or butter

1 pound pork boneless center loin roast, cut into 2 × 1/4-inch strips

8 flour tortillas (8 or 10 inches in diameter), warmed (page 42)

1 cup shredded Monterey Jack cheese (4 ounces)

2 tablespoons margarine or butter, melted

Prepare Pineapple Salsa; reserve. Heat 1 tablespoon margarine in 10-inch skillet over medium heat until hot and bubbly. Cook pork in margarine about 10 minutes, stirring occasionally, until no longer pink in center; drain.

Heat oven to 425°. Spoon about 1/4 cup of the pork onto half of each tortilla; top with about 2 tablespoons of the cheese. Fold tortilla in half over filling. Arrange 4 of the filled tortillas in ungreased jelly roll pan, 15 1/2 × 10 1/2 × 1 inch; brush with melted margarine. Bake about 10 minutes or until light golden brown. Repeat with remaining tacos. Serve with salsa.

1 Serving: Calories 640 (Calories from Fat 305); Fat 34g (Saturated 13g); Cholesterol 95 mg; Sodium 800 mg; Carbohydrate 51g (Dietary Fiber 2g); Protein 35g

Breakfast Tacos

6 SERVINGS

As colorful as a Mexican serape or blanket, this dish is sure to become a weekend favorite.

4 eggs

1/4 teaspoon garlic salt

1/4 teaspoon pepper

1/4 cup chopped green bell pepper

1/4 cup chopped green onions (3 medium)

1 tablespoon margarine or butter

1/2 cup shredded Monterey Jack cheese with jalapeño peppers (2 ounces)

6 taco shells

1 cup shredded lettuce

1 small avocado, sliced (about 3/4 cup)

1/4 cup thick-and-chunky salsa

Stir eggs, garlic salt and pepper thoroughly with fork. Stir in bell pepper and onions. Melt margarine in 8-inch skillet over medium heat. Pour egg mixture into skillet.

As mixture begins to set at bottom and side, gently lift cooked portions with spatula so that thin, uncooked portions can flow to bottom. Avoid constant stirring. Cook 3 to 4 minutes or until eggs are thickened throughout. Gently stir in cheese.

Heat taco shells as directed on package. Place lettuce in taco shells. Spoon eggs onto lettuce. Top with avocado and salsa.

1 Serving: Calories 215 (Calories from Fat 145); Fat 16g (Saturated 4g); Cholesterol 150 mg; Sodium 280 mg; Carbohydrate 13g (Dietary Fiber 3g); Protein 8g

Fresh Fruit Frappé (page 110);
Mexican Coffee (page 115); Breakfast Tacos

Crab Tostadas

4 SERVINGS

Fresh lime juice is often the touch that distinguishes a distinctly Mexican dish.

1 can (6 ounces) frozen guacamole, thawed

2/3 cup chopped tomato

1 tablespoon canned chopped green chilies

1 tablespoon lime juice

1/4 teaspoon pepper

4 tostada shells

1 cup shredded lettuce

1 can (6 ounces) crabmeat, drained and cartilage removed, or 3/4 cup shredded imitation crabmeat

2 green onions, sliced

4 lime wedges

Mix guacamole, tomato, chilies, lime juice and pepper. Heat tostada shells as directed on package. Top with lettuce, guacamole mixture and crabmeat. Sprinkle with onions. Serve with lime wedges.

1 Serving: Calories 215 (Calories from Fat 65); Fat 7g (Saturated 1g); Cholesterol 30 mg; Sodium 480 mg; Carbohydrate 29g (Dietary Fiber 3g); Protein 12g

Black Bean and Beef Tostadas

6 SERVINGS

A tostada is an open-face sandwich. Ingredients typically offer contrasts of soft and crisp, hot and cold, spicy and mild.

1/2 pound ground beef

1 medium onion, chopped (1/2 cup)

1 can (10 ounces) chopped tomatoes and green chilies, undrained

1 can (15 ounces) black beans, rinsed and drained

6 tostada shells

1 cup shredded lettuce

2/3 cup chopped tomato

3/4 cup shredded Colby-Monterey Jack cheese (3 ounces)

Cook beef and onion in 10-inch skillet over medium-high heat, stirring occasionally, until beef is brown; drain. Stir in tomatoes. Heat to boiling; reduce heat to low. Simmer uncovered about 10 minutes or until liquid has evaporated. Stir in beans.

Heat tostada shells as directed on package. Top tostada shells with bean mixture, lettuce, tomato and cheese.

1 Serving: Calories 360 (Calories from Fat 125); Fat 14g (Saturated 6g); Cholesterol 35 mg; Sodium 530 mg; Carbohydrate 44g (Dietary Fiber 6g); Protein 20g

Black Bean and Beef Tostadas

TORTILLA SANDWICHES

If you're "sandwiched" in a sliced-bread rut, break away and try tortillas. Tortilla sandwiches are easy to make, fun to eat and the combinations are endless.

1. Start with: 8- or 10-inch flour tortillas.

2. Spread with any of the following:

- Mayonnaise mixed with taco seasoning mix
- Guacamole
- Cream cheese spread with olives
- Processed cheese spread

3. Top with any of the following:

- Thinly sliced smoked turkey, regular turkey, roast beef, roast pork or ham
- Shredded Cheddar, Colby-Monterey Jack, or Monterey Jack cheese
- Shredded lettuce, carrots, jicama or zucchini
- Jalapeño pepper rings, sliced ripe olives, chopped onion, chopped tomatoes or canned corn, drained
- Sour cream, guacamole or salsa

4. Roll up and serve.

Mixed Tostadas

6 SERVINGS

Vegetable oil

6 corn tortillas (5 or 6 inches in diameter)

1 can (16 ounces) refried beans, heated

1 jar (10 ounces) thick-and-chunky salsa (about 1 1/2 cups)

2 cups cut-up cooked chicken

3/4 cup shredded Monterey Jack cheese (3 ounces)

3 cups shredded lettuce

1 avocado, cut into 12 slices

Sour cream

Heat 1/8 inch oil in 10-inch skillet over medium heat just until hot. Cook 1 tortilla at a time in oil about 1 minute or until crisp; drain.

Spread each tortilla with 1/4 cup of the beans. Top with 2 tablespoons of the salsa, 1/3 cup of the chicken and 2 more tablespoons of the salsa. Sprinkle with cheese.

Set oven control to broil. Place tortillas on rack in broiler pan. Broil with tops 2 to 3 inches from heat about 3 minutes or until cheese is melted. Top with lettuce, avocado slices and sour cream.

1 Serving: Calories 385 (Calories from Fat 190); Fat 21g (Saturated 8g); Cholesterol 60 mg; Sodium 770 mg; Carbohydrate 32g (Dietary Fiber 8g); Protein 25g

Chicken Fajitas

4 SERVINGS

1 pound boneless, skinless chicken breasts

2 tablespoons orange juice

2 teaspoons vegetable oil

1 teaspoon chili powder

1/4 teaspoon salt

1/4 teaspoon pepper

1 clove garlic, finely chopped

Chile Sour Cream (right)

4 flour tortillas (8 or 10 inches in diameter)

1 medium onion, sliced

1 medium green or red bell pepper, cut into 1/4-inch strips

Chopped fresh cilantro or parsley

Cut chicken crosswise into 1/4-inch slices. (Chicken is easier to cut if partially frozen, about 1 1/2 hours.) Mix orange juice, oil, chili powder, salt, pepper and garlic in medium glass or plastic bowl or large, resealable heavy-duty plastic bag. Add chicken; toss to coat. Cover bowl or seal bag and refrigerate at least 4 hours but no longer than 24 hours, turning chicken occasionally. Prepare Chile Sour Cream.

Remove chicken from marinade. Heat 10-inch nonstick skillet over high heat. Cook chicken in skillet 3 minutes, stirring occasionally. Stir in onion and bell pepper. Cook 3 to 4 minutes, stirring occasionally, until vegetables are crisp-tender.

Place one-fourth of the chicken mixture and 2 tablespoons Chile Sour Cream on center of each tortilla. Sprinkle with cilantro. Fold one end of tortilla up about 1 inch over chicken mixture; fold right and left sides over folded end, overlapping. Fold remaining end down.

Chile Sour Cream

1/2 cup sour cream

2 tablespoons orange juice

2 teaspoons chopped seeded jalapeño chilies

1/4 teaspoon ground cumin

Mix all ingredients. Cover and refrigerate at least 1 hour to blend flavors.

1 Serving: Calories 405 (Calories from Fat 135); Fat 15g (Saturated 6g); Cholesterol 105 mg; Sodium 440 mg; Carbohydrate 31g (Dietary Fiber 2g); Protein 39g

Southwest Beef Fajitas

8 SERVINGS

1 pound beef boneless top round steak, about 1/2 inch thick

1/4 cup lime juice

2 tablespoons vegetable oil

2 teaspoons chili powder

2 cloves garlic, finely chopped

Corn-Olive Salsa (page 24)

Quick Guacamole (page 20)

8 flour tortillas (8 or 10 inches in diameter), warmed (page 42)

Cut beef diagonally across grain into thin slices, each 2 × 1/8 inch. (Beef is easier to cut if partially frozen, about 1 1/2 hours.) Mix lime juice, oil, chili powder and garlic in medium glass or plastic bowl or large, resealable heavy-duty plastic bag. Add beef; toss to coat with marinade. Cover bowl or seal bag and refrigerate 1 hour. Meanwhile, prepare Corn-Olive Salsa and Quick Guacamole; refrigerate until ready to assemble fajitas.

Set oven control to broil. Remove beef from marinade; discard marinade. Place beef slices on rack in broiler pan. Broil 2 to 3 inches from heat about 5 minutes or until brown.

Place one-eighth of the beef and some of the salsa and guacamole on center of each tortilla. Fold one end of tortilla up about 1 inch over beef mixture; fold right and left sides over folded end, overlapping. Fold remaining end down. Serve with remaining salsa and guacamole.

1 Serving: Calories 265 (Calories from Fat 100); Fat 11g (Saturated 2g); Cholesterol 25 mg; Sodium 350 mg; Carbohydrate 29g (Dietary Fiber 2g); Protein 14g

Grilled Vegetable Tortillas

6 SERVINGS

1/2 cup diced red bell pepper

1/2 cup diced yellow bell pepper

1/2 cup diced chayote or zucchini

6 flour tortillas (8 or 10 inches in diameter)

1 1/2 cups shredded Colby-Monterey Jack cheese (6 ounces)

1 tablespoon margarine or butter

Mix bell peppers and chayote. Spoon about 1/4 cup of the vegetable mixture down center of each tortilla. Top with 1/4 cup of the cheese. Fold tortilla into thirds over filling.

Melt margarine in 10-inch skillet over medium heat. Place 3 filled tortillas at a time, seam sides down, in margarine. Cook about 6 minutes, turning after 3 minutes, until golden brown.

1 Serving: Calories 265 (Calories from Fat 125); Fat 14g (Saturated 7g); Cholesterol 30 mg; Sodium 400 mg; Carbohydrate 25g (Dietary Fiber 1g); Protein 11g

Grilled Vegetable Tortillas

Tortillas

Tortillas are round, flat unleavened breads made from ground wheat or corn and are the basis of Mexican cookery. In Mexico, freshly made tortillas or fresh corn tortilla dough can be purchased from a *tortilleria* or street vendors. Freshly made tortillas and dough are difficult to find in the United States, but your best bet would be checking Hispanic or Latin grocery stores or mail-order sources.

Tortillas are wonderfully versatile. They can be folded, rolled, stacked, stuffed, used as dippers, fried crisp, munched fresh and can be eaten at any meal. In northern Mexico, where wheat crops are abundant, flour tortillas predominate and in the south, corn crops flourish, so corn tortillas are more common. The humble tortilla is found in some of the most well-known and loved Mexican dishes:

- A *burrito* is a flour tortilla folded like an envelope around a filling.

- *Chilaquiles* is a casserole of fried flour or corn tortilla chips, baked or cooked in a skillet with sauces and fillings.

- A *chimichanga* is a burrito that traditionally is deep-fat fried after filling.

- An *enchilada* is a filled corn tortilla served with a special tomato sauce.

- *Fajitas* are flour tortillas filled with slices of beef or chicken, onions and bell peppers.

- A *flauta* (flute) is a very tightly rolled enchilada. Sometimes flautas are deep-fat fried.

- *Nachos* are crisp chips of flour or corn tortillas served with cheese, salsa or chilies and often meats, olives, sour cream and guacamole. Nachos are usually served as an appetizer.

- A *quesadilla* is a flour or corn tortilla, usually filled with cheese, then folded or stacked.

- And, a *taco* is a usually a corn tortilla, crisp or soft, folded in half with a filling.

Types of Tortillas

Corn tortillas are traditionally made from fresh *masa*, meaning "dough." Masa is made from dried field corn that has been cooked, soaked in lime and ground. In the traditional manner, masa was ground by hand using a grinding stone called a *metate* or *mano*. Today tortilla production is mechanized for commercial production. For the sake of convenience and greater availability, an instant *masa harina* flour mix (also called instant corn flour tortilla mix) can be found in Hispanic or Latin markets or in most large supermarkets. This instant mix is made from fresh masa that has been dehydrated. Don't be tempted to use cornmeal in place of the instant mix. Because cornmeal is so coarse, the tortillas would be crumbly and dry. Freshly made tortillas are formed by patting them out by hand or are flattened with a tortilla press. A rolling pin will also work.

Fortunately, for those of us not willing to make tortillas from scratch, prepackaged corn tortillas are easily found and are generally available in the 5- or 6-inch diameter size.

Flour tortillas are traditionally made from white, all-purpose flour, water, salt and lard or shortening. Some recipes call for leavening such as baking powder, but it isn't necessary for successful results. The Mexican term for flour is *harina de trigo*, and the term for flour tortilla dough is *masa de trigo*. Whole wheat flour is sometimes used, and trendy southwestern chefs and entrepreneurs, influenced by the staples of Mexican cooking, are making both savory and sweet-flavored flour tortillas, such as jalapeño, pumpkin and cinnamon.

As with corn tortillas, flour tortillas are traditionally patted out by hand, with great pride taken in producing thin, evenly round tortillas. Tortilla presses are available, and a rolling pin works equally well. Prepackaged flour tortillas are widely available and come in many widths, usually eight to twelve inches in diameter.

Selecting and Storing

Selecting: Check on freshness by gently bending the tortilla package. The tortillas should be somewhat flexible (corn tortillas, however, are not as soft as flour tortillas) and should not crack. Check the edges of the tortillas to be certain they are not dry or cracked.

Storing: Store in the refrigerator for up to one week. Once opened, tortillas must be tightly wrapped to prevent drying. Or, store tightly wrapped in the freezer for up to two months. Thaw frozen tortillas in the refrigerator overnight.

(Continued on next page)

Heating and Softening Tortillas

Heating tortillas makes them flexible and easier to handle when rolling. This is especially true for corn tortillas, which are not as soft and tender as those made from flour. Additionally, warm tortillas served plain or with butter are a delicious accompaniment to soup, chili, salads or grilled meats.

Oven Method: Heat oven to 250°. Wrap desired number of tortillas tightly in aluminum foil. Heat for 15 minutes.

Stove-top Method: Warm tortillas one at a time in an ungreased skillet or griddle over medium-high heat, turning frequently until warm.

Microwave Method: Place two tortillas at a time between dampened microwaveable paper towels or microwaveable plastic wrap and microwave on high for 15 to 20 seconds or until warm.

Keeping Tortillas Warm: To keep tortillas warm during a meal, place them in a tortilla holder with a lid, or wrap in aluminum foil and place in a tortilla basket or decorative basket. Also, a clay warming stone, which can be purchased in most housewares departments, can be heated and placed in the bottom of the basket to help retain heat.

To keep tortillas warm for several hours, wrap warm tortillas tightly in aluminum foil; then wrap in a thick kitchen towel and then in several layers of newspaper.

Spinach-Cheese Tortilla Rolls

4 SERVINGS

This is a delicious meatless main dish. For entertaining, double the recipe and refrigerate overnight; increase baking time to 45 minutes.

1 can (15 ounces) chunky Mexican-style
    tomato sauce

3 tablespoons chopped fresh cilantro or
    parsley

1 package (10 ounces) frozen chopped
    spinach, thawed and squeezed to drain

1 cup ricotta cheese

1 egg, beaten

1/8 teaspoon red pepper sauce

4 flour tortillas (8 or 10 inches in diameter)

1/2 cup shredded Cheddar cheese (2 ounces)

1 tablespoon chopped fresh cilantro or
    parsley

Heat oven to 375°. Grease square baking dish, 9 × 9 × 2 inches. Mix tomato sauce and 3 tablespoons cilantro in 1-quart saucepan. Heat to boiling; reduce heat to low. Simmer uncovered 5 minutes.

Mix spinach, ricotta cheese, egg and pepper sauce. Spoon 1/2 cup of the spinach mixture down center of each tortilla. Roll up tortilla; place seam side down in dish. Spoon tomato sauce over tortillas. Sprinkle with cheese. Bake uncovered about 30 minutes or until heated through. Sprinkle with 1 tablespoon cilantro.

1 Serving: Calories 370 (Calories from Fat 160); Fat 18g (Saturated 8g); Cholesterol 85 mg; Sodium 790 mg; Carbohydrate 37g (Dietary Fiber 3g); Protein 18g

Corn and Crab Quesadillas

6 SERVINGS

Corn is a staple of the Mexican diet. It is used fresh in many dishes or is dried and ground into masa for tortillas.

1 package (8 ounces) cream cheese, softened

1 can (11 ounces) whole kernel corn,
    drained

1/2 cup chopped fresh cilantro or parsley

1/3 cup chopped green onions (4 medium)

1 jar (2 ounces) diced pimientos, drained

1/2 teaspoon pepper

1/4 teaspoon ground red pepper (cayenne)

1 pound chopped cooked crabmeat or
    imitation crabmeat (about 2 cups)

6 flour tortillas (8 or 10 inches in diameter)

1 tablespoon margarine or butter, melted

Sour cream and chopped fresh cilantro, if
    desired

Mix cream cheese, corn, cilantro, onions, pimientos, pepper and red pepper in medium bowl. Fold in crabmeat. Spread 2/3 cup of the crabmeat mixture over each tortilla; fold tortilla in half, pressing lightly. Brush both sides of each tortilla with margarine.

Cook 3 tortillas at a time in 12-inch skillet over medium-high heat about 5 minutes, turning once, until light brown. Garnish with sour cream and cilantro.

1 Serving: Calories 400 (Calories from Fat 180); Fat 20g (Saturated 10g); Cholesterol 120 mg; Sodium 690 mg; Carbohydrate 34g (Dietary Fiber 2g); Protein 23g

Chicken Chilaquiles Casserole

6 SERVINGS

1/2 cup vegetable oil

10 flour or corn tortillas (6 or 8 inches in diameter), cut into 1/2-inch strips

2 cups shredded cooked chicken or turkey

1 jar (16 ounces) green salsa (salsa verde) or salsa (about 2 cups)

2 cups shredded mozzarella or Monterey Jack cheese (8 ounces)

Heat oil in 10-inch skillet over medium-high heat. Cook tortilla strips in oil 30 to 60 seconds, stirring occasionally, until light golden brown. Remove with slotted spoon and drain on paper towels.

Heat oven to 350°. Grease 2-quart casserole. Arrange half of the tortilla strips in bottom of casserole. Top with chicken, 3/4 cup of the salsa and 1 cup of the cheese. Gently press layers down into casserole. Repeat with remaining tortilla strips, salsa and cheese. Bake uncovered about 30 minutes or until cheese is melted and golden brown.

1 Serving: Calories 555 (Calories from Fat 260); Fat 29g (Saturated 8g); Cholesterol 60 mg; Sodium 1020 mg; Carbohydrate 45g (Dietary Fiber 3g); Protein 31g

Tortilla Skillet

4 SERVINGS

1/2 cup vegetable oil

12 corn or flour tortillas (6 or 8 inches in diameter), cut into 1/2-inch strips

1/2 cup chopped green onions (5 medium)

1 clove garlic, finely chopped

1 can (16 ounces) whole tomatoes, drained

1/2 teaspoon dried oregano leaves

1/2 teaspoon salt

1/8 teaspoon pepper

1 cup shredded Monterey Jack cheese (4 ounces)

Sour cream

Heat oil in 10-inch skillet over medium-high heat. Cook tortilla strips, onions and garlic in oil 30 to 60 seconds, stirring occasionally, until strips are light golden brown. Remove with slotted spoon and drain on paper towels. Drain oil into heatproof container and refrigerate for another use.

Mix tortilla strips, tomatoes, oregano, salt and pepper in same skillet, breaking up tomatoes. Sprinkle with cheese. Heat just until cheese is melted. Serve with sour cream.

1 Serving: Calories 440 (Calories from Fat 245); Fat 27g (Saturated 10g); Cholesterol 35 mg; Sodium 760 mg; Carbohydrate 42g (Dietary Fiber 5g); Protein 12g

Tortilla Skillet

Seafood Chilaquiles Casserole

6 SERVINGS

1/2 cup vegetable oil

10 flour or corn tortillas (6 or 8 inches in diameter), cut into 1/2-inch strips

1/4 cup (1/2 stick) margarine or butter

1/2 cup sliced green onions (5 medium)

1/4 cup all-purpose flour

1/2 teaspoon salt

1/4 teaspoon pepper

2 cups half-and-half

1 canned chipotle chile in adobo sauce, finely chopped

1 pound bay scallops

1 pound uncooked peeled and deveined medium shrimp

4 slices bacon, crisply cooked and crumbled

Heat oil in 10-inch skillet over medium-high heat. Cook tortilla strips in oil 30 to 60 seconds, stirring occasionally, until light golden brown. Remove with slotted spoon and drain on paper towels.

Melt margarine in 3-quart saucepan over low heat. Cook onions in margarine, stirring occasionally, until tender. Stir in flour, salt and pepper. Cook, stirring constantly, until mixture is bubbly; remove from heat. Stir in half-and-half. Heat to boiling, stirring constantly. Boil and stir 1 minute; reduce heat to medium-low. Stir in chile, scallops and shrimp. Cook over medium heat about 9 minutes, stirring frequently, just until shrimp are pink.

Heat oven to 350°. Grease 3-quart casserole. Arrange half of the tortilla strips in bottom of casserole. Top with half of the seafood mixture. Repeat with remaining tortilla strips and seafood mixture. Top with bacon. Bake uncovered 15 to 20 minutes or until hot and bubbly.

1 Serving: Calories 705 (Calories from Fat 350); Fat 39g (Saturated 11g); Cholesterol 165 mg; Sodium 1090 mg; Carbohydrate 51g (Dietary Fiber 2g); Protein 39g

UNFRIED TORTILLA BASKETS

Tortilla baskets make fun holders for salsas, sauces, dips, spreads and ice cream, too. We've developed an easy and clever way to prepare them that eliminates deep-fat frying.

Edible tortilla baskets are simple to make in the oven. For each basket, invert a 6-ounce custard cup onto a cookie sheet, and spray with nonstick cooking spray. Place one 8- to 10-inch flour tortilla over each custard cup. Bake at 400° for 5 to 8 minutes or until crisp. Remove from the custard cups and cool. They're ideal containers for Cinnamon "Fried" Ice Cream (page 102). The best part is you can eat them!

Beef Tortilla Casserole

8 SERVINGS

1/2 cup vegetable oil

10 corn tortillas (5 or 6 inches in diameter), cut into 2-inch strips

1 pound ground beef

2 Anaheim or jalapeño chilies, seeded and finely chopped

1 medium onion, chopped (1/2 cup)

1 jar (16 ounces) salsa or picante sauce (about 2 cups)

1 can (15 to 16 ounces) pinto beans, rinsed and drained

2 cups shredded Cheddar cheese (8 ounces)

Guacamole and sour cream, if desired

Heat oil in 10-inch skillet over medium-high heat. Cook tortilla strips in oil 30 to 60 seconds, stirring occasionally, until light golden brown. Remove with slotted spoon and drain on paper towels. Drain oil into a heatproof container and refrigerate for another use.

Cook beef, chilies and onion in same skillet over medium-high heat, stirring occasionally, until beef is brown; drain.

Heat oven to 350°. Grease rectangular baking dish, 13 × 9 × 2 inches. Arrange tortilla strips in bottom of dish. Top with beef mixture, salsa, beans and cheese. Bake uncovered 25 to 30 minutes or until hot and bubbly. Serve with guacamole and sour cream.

1 Serving: Calories 425 (Calories from Fat 225); Fat 25g (Saturated 10g); Cholesterol 60 mg; Sodium 700 mg; Carbohydrate 33g (Dietary Fiber 7g); Protein 24g

Spicy Mexican Torte

8 SERVINGS

1/2 pound chorizo or spicy pork sausage links, chopped

1 large onion, chopped (1 cup)

2 cloves garlic, finely chopped

1 can (4 ounces) chopped green chilies, drained

8 flour tortillas (8 or 10 inches in diameter)

2 cups shredded Monterey Jack cheese or Monterey Jack cheese with jalapeño peppers (8 ounces)

1 can (16 ounces) refried beans

1 jar (7 ounces) roasted red bell peppers, drained

Salsa, sour cream or guacamole, if desired

Cook sausage, onion and garlic in 10-inch skillet over medium heat, stirring occasionally, until sausage is brown; drain. Stir in chilies.

Heat oven to 400°. Grease pie plate, 10 × 1 1/2 inches. Place 2 tortillas in pie plate. Spread half of the sausage mixture over tortillas. Sprinkle with half of the cheese. Place 2 tortillas on cheese. Spread with beans. Place 2 tortillas on beans. Place peppers on tortillas. Place 2 tortillas on peppers. Spread with remaining sausage mixture. Sprinkle with remaining cheese.

Cover and bake 40 minutes. Uncover and bake about 15 minutes longer or until cheese is melted and center is hot. Cool 10 minutes before cutting. Serve with salsa.

1 Serving: Calories 425 (Calories from Fat 205); Fat 23g (Saturated 11g); Cholesterol 50 mg; Sodium 1100 mg; Carbohydrate 39g (Dietary Fiber 5g); Protein 21g

3

Rice, Beans and Soup

Chili con Carne with Tomatoes (page 59)

Southwest Green Rice

6 SERVINGS

2 large poblano chilies or 1 medium green bell pepper, roasted (page 18)

2 cloves garlic, finely chopped

1 medium onion, chopped (1/2 cup)

1 cup uncooked regular long grain rice

2 cups chicken broth

1/4 teaspoon salt

1/4 cup chopped fresh parsley

Place chilies, garlic and onion in food processor or blender. Cover and process until smooth.

Mix chile mixture and remaining ingredients except parsley in 3-quart saucepan. Heat to boiling, stirring once or twice; reduce heat to low. Cover and simmer 16 minutes. (Do not lift cover or stir.) Remove from heat; fluff rice lightly with fork. Cover and let steam 10 minutes. Stir in parsley.

1 Serving: Calories 135 (Calories from Fat 10); Fat 1g (Saturated 0g); Cholesterol 0 mg; Sodium 350 mg; Carbohydrate 29g (Dietary Fiber 1g); Protein 4g

Mexican Red Rice

8 SERVINGS

Seasoned rice is frequently part of a Mexican meal. This one is made quickly and easily by using instant rice.

1 tablespoon vegetable oil

1 medium onion, chopped (1/2 cup)

1 small green bell pepper, chopped (1/2 cup)

1 clove garlic, finely chopped

1 can (10 1/2 ounces) condensed beef broth

1 can (8 ounces) tomato sauce

3/4 teaspoon ground cumin

3/4 teaspoon chili powder

2 1/4 cups uncooked instant rice

Heat oil in 2-quart saucepan over medium-high heat. Cook onion, bell pepper and garlic in oil, stirring occasionally, until vegetables are tender. Stir in broth, tomato sauce, cumin and chili powder.

Heat to boiling; stir in rice. Cover and cook over very low heat about 10 minutes or until liquid is absorbed. Fluff with fork.

1 Serving: Calories 220 (Calories from Fat 20); Fat 2g (Saturated 0g); Cholesterol 0 mg; Sodium 370 mg; Carbohydrate 46g (Dietary Fiber 1g); Protein 6g

Mexican Red Rice

Baked Rice with Green Chilies

8 SERVINGS

To reduce calories and fat, use low-fat or fat-free sour cream and reduced-fat cheeses.

3 cups cooked white rice

1 cup sour cream

1/2 cup shredded Monterey Jack cheese (2 ounces)

1/2 cup shredded Cheddar cheese (2 ounces)

1 to 2 teaspoons chili powder

2 cans (4 ounces each) chopped green chilies, drained

Heat oven to 350°. Mix all ingredients in ungreased 2-quart casserole. Bake uncovered 30 minutes.

1 Serving: Calories 190 (Calories from Fat 90); Fat 10g (Saturated 6g); Cholesterol 35 mg; Sodium 580 mg; Carbohydrate 19g (Dietary Fiber 0g); Protein 6g

Mexican Cinnamon Rice

6 SERVINGS

2 tablespoons margarine or butter

1 medium onion, chopped (1/2 cup)

1 clove garlic, finely chopped

1 cup uncooked regular long grain rice

1/2 cup currants

2 1/4 cups chicken broth

2 teaspoons ground cinnamon

1/4 teaspoon salt

1 to 2 tablespoons chopped fresh cilantro

Melt margarine in 3-quart saucepan over medium-high heat. Cook onion and garlic in margarine, stirring occasionally, until onion is tender.

Stir in remaining ingredients except cilantro. Heat to boiling, stirring once or twice; reduce heat to low. Cover and simmer 16 minutes. (Do not lift cover or stir.) Remove from heat; fluff rice lightly with fork. Cover and let steam 10 minutes. Stir in cilantro.

1 Serving: Calories 210 (Calories from Fat 45); Fat 5g (Saturated 1g); Cholesterol 0 mg; Sodium 430 mg; Carbohydrate 37g (Dietary Fiber 1g); Protein 5g

Pine Nut and Green Onion Pilaf

6 SERVINGS

2 tablespoons margarine or butter

1 cup uncooked regular long grain rice

1/2 cup sliced green onions (5 medium)

1/2 cup pine nuts

2 1/2 cups chicken broth

1 teaspoon grated lemon peel

1/4 teaspoon salt

1/4 cup sliced green onion tops

Melt margarine in 3-quart saucepan over medium-high heat. Cook rice, 1/2 cup onions and the nuts in margarine about 5 minutes, stirring occasionally, until nuts are light brown.

Stir in broth, lemon peel and salt. Heat to boiling, stirring once or twice; reduce heat to low. Cover and simmer 14 minutes; remove from heat. Fluff rice lightly with fork. Cover and let steam 5 to 10 minutes. Sprinkle with onion tops.

1 Serving: Calories 225 (Calories from Fat 100); Fat 11g (Saturated 2g); Cholesterol 0 mg; Sodium 470 mg; Carbohydrate 28g (Dietary Fiber 2g); Protein 6g

Río Grande Rice and Beans

6 SERVINGS

For richest flavor, use a fully ripe avocado that yields to gentle pressure.

1 can (10 1/2 ounces) condensed chicken broth

1 1/3 cups uncooked instant rice

1/4 teaspoon pepper

1 can (15 to 16 ounces) kidney beans, rinsed and drained

1/3 cup sliced green onions (4 medium)

1 medium avocado, diced

2 teaspoons lime juice

1 green onion, sliced

Heat broth to boiling in 2-quart saucepan. Stir in rice and pepper; remove from heat. Cover and let steam about 5 minutes or until liquid is absorbed. Fluff with fork. Stir in beans and 1/3 cup onions.

Mix avocado and lime juice in glass or plastic bowl; gently fold into rice. Garnish with sliced onion.

1 Serving: Calories 255 (Calories from Fat 55); Fat 6g (Saturated 1g); Cholesterol 0 mg; Sodium 530 mg; Carbohydrate 46g (Dietary Fiber 5g); Protein 9g

RICE

Mexican cooking generally uses regular, long grain white rice. Rice is a staple in many recipes and is a common side dish. Many of the recipes in this book call for cooked rice and we have provided a foolproof cooking method below:

1. In 2-quart saucepan, combine 2 cups water with 1 cup regular, long grain white rice.

2. Heat rice and water to boiling. Reduce heat to low. Cover and simmer 15 minutes until rice is tender and water is absorbed.

3. Yield: 3 cups cooked rice.

4. Cooked rice can be stored tightly covered in the refrigerator for up to 5 days or frozen in a tightly covered container for up to 6 months.

Red-Hot Rice Ideas

- Chicken, beef, vegetable or tomato juice can be substituted for the water.

- Chili powder, crushed red pepper, chopped green onions, bell peppers or chilies can be added with rice and cooking liquid.

- For a superquick, zesty side dish, combine hot cooked rice with your favorite salsa. To dress it up, garnish with sliced ripe olives and shredded Cheddar cheese.

- For easy, cheesy rice, combine hot cooked rice with melted processed cheese spread.

Frijoles Blancos

5 SERVINGS

Canned beans are an excellent nutritional value—low in fat and high in protein and fiber.

- 1 can (15 ounces) chunky Mexican-style tomato sauce
- 1 1/4 teaspoons ground cumin
- 1/8 teaspoon pepper
- 1 can (15 to 16 ounces) navy beans, rinsed and drained
- 1 tablespoon chopped fresh cilantro or parsley

Mix tomato sauce, cumin and pepper in 2-quart saucepan. Heat to boiling; reduce heat to medium. Cook uncovered 5 minutes. Stir in beans. Cook 4 to 5 minutes or until beans are heated. Sprinkle with cilantro.

1 Serving: Calories 145 (Calories from Fat 35); Fat 4g (Saturated 1g); Cholesterol 0 mg; Sodium 470 mg; Carbohydrate 26g (Dietary Fiber 6g); Protein 7g

Frontier Beans

6 SERVINGS

- 1 cup sliced green onions (9 medium)
- 1/2 pound chorizo or spicy pork sausage links, chopped
- 2 cans (15 to 16 ounces each) pinto beans, 1 can drained
- 3 small poblano chilies, roasted and chopped (page 18), or 1 can (4 ounces) chopped green chilies, drained
- 1 large tomato, chopped (1 cup)
- 1/4 teaspoon salt

Heat oven to 350°. Cook onions and sausage in 10-inch skillet over medium-high heat, stirring occasionally, until sausage is brown; drain.

Mix sausage mixture and remaining ingredients in ungreased 2-quart casserole. Bake uncovered about 30 minutes or until hot and bubbly.

1 Serving: Calories 325 (Calories from Fat 135); Fat 15g (Saturated 6g); Cholesterol 35 mg; Sodium 860 mg; Carbohydrate 37g (Dietary Fiber 9g); Protein 20g

Frontier Beans

CHEESE

Cheese became a distinctive ingredient in Mexican cooking with the introduction of cows and goats by the Spaniards. Many varieties are used for stuffing, layering and topping in recipes.

Storage

- Store cheese in the refrigerator. Wrap it tightly in aluminum foil or plastic wrap to prevent moisture loss.

- Firm cheeses such as Cheddar keep 2 months or more; semisoft cheeses such as Monterey Jack keep about 3 weeks; and soft cheeses such as cream cheese keep about 2 weeks.

- If mold forms on cheese other than blue and Roquefort cheeses, which are mold-ripened, cut it off. If mold has penetrated cheese, discard the cheese.

- Freeze cheese tightly wrapped in moistureproof freezer wrap for up to 3 months. Thaw in refrigerator rather than at room temperature to prevent excessive crumbling. Cheese that has been frozen works best in baked recipes or recipes in which the cheese should melt. Frozen cheese generally becomes crumbly, preventing smooth, evenly cut slices.

For a specific listing of types of cheese and their descriptions, refer to the glossary (pages 117–118).

Spicy Garbanzos

6 SERVINGS

1 tablespoon vegetable oil
1 teaspoon whole mustard seed
1 medium onion, chopped (1/2 cup)
1/2 cup chicken broth
2 tablespoons tomato paste
1/2 teaspoon salt
1/4 teaspoon ground cinnamon
1/8 teaspoon ground cloves
2 cans (15 to 16 ounces each) garbanzo beans, rinsed and drained

Heat oil in 2-quart saucepan over medium-high heat. Cook mustard seed and onion in oil, stirring constantly, until onion is tender.

Stir in remaining ingredients. Cook about 5 minutes, stirring occasionally, until beans are heated through.

1 Serving: Calories 175 (Calories from Fat 45); Fat 5g (Saturated 1g); Cholesterol 0 mg; Sodium 520 mg; Carbohydrate 29g (Dietary Fiber 6g); Protein 9g

Refried Black Beans

6 SERVINGS

2 tablespoons vegetable oil

1 small onion, chopped (1/4 cup)

2 jalapeño chilies, seeded and finely chopped

2 cloves garlic, finely chopped

2 cans (15 ounces each) black beans, undrained

1 canned chipotle chile in adobo sauce, chopped

1 teaspoon chili powder

1/2 teaspoon salt

Heat oil in 10-inch skillet over medium-high heat. Cook onion, jalapeño chilies and garlic in oil, stirring occasionally, until onion is tender.

Stir in remaining ingredients; mash beans. Cook uncovered about 15 minutes, stirring occasionally, until thickened.

1 Serving: Calories 230 (Calories from Fat 55); Fat 6g (Saturated 1g); Cholesterol 0 mg; Sodium 620 mg; Carbohydrate 41g (Dietary Fiber 10g); Protein 13g

Frijoles Rancheros

6 SERVINGS

8 slices bacon, cut up

2 jalapeño chilies, seeded and chopped

2 cloves garlic, finely chopped

1 large onion, chopped (1 cup)

3/4 cup beer or beef broth

1 tablespoon white vinegar

2 to 3 teaspoons chili powder

2 cans (15 to 16 ounces each) pinto beans, drained

1 can (6 ounces) tomato paste

Heat oven to 375°. Cook bacon in 10-inch skillet over medium-high heat until crisp. Stir in chilies, garlic and onion. Cook, stirring occasionally, until onion is tender; drain.

Mix bacon mixture and remaining ingredients in ungreased 2-quart casserole. Bake uncovered about 45 minutes, stirring once, until hot and bubbly.

1 Serving: Calories 230 (Calories from Fat 45); Fat 5g (Saturated 2g); Cholesterol 5 mg; Sodium 670 mg; Carbohydrate 43g (Dietary Fiber 11g); Protein 14g

Marinated Black-Eyed Peas

8 SERVINGS

2 cans (15 to 16 ounces each) black-eyed peas, drained

2 medium stalks celery, chopped (1 cup)

1 small green bell pepper, chopped (1/2 cup)

1 jalapeño chile, seeded and chopped

1/2 cup chopped red onion

1/4 cup olive or vegetable oil

2 tablespoons red wine vinegar

1/4 teaspoon salt

1/8 teaspoon pepper

1 clove garlic, crushed

Mix peas, celery, bell pepper, chile and onion in large glass or plastic bowl. Mix remaining ingredients; pour over pea mixture. Cover and refrigerate at least 2 hours but no longer than 24 hours, stirring occasionally.

1 Serving: Calories 145 (Calories from Fat 65); Fat 7g (Saturated 1g); Cholesterol 0 mg; Sodium 300 mg; Carbohydrate 22g (Dietary Fiber 9g); Protein 7g

Chili con Carne with Tomatoes

4 SERVINGS (ABOUT 1 CUP EACH)

1 pound ground beef

1 large onion, chopped (1 cup)

1 medium green bell pepper, chopped (1 cup)

1 can (28 ounces) whole tomatoes, undrained

1 can (8 ounces) tomato sauce

2 teaspoons chili powder

1 teaspoon salt

1/8 teaspoon ground red pepper (cayenne)

1/8 teaspoon paprika

1 can (15 to 16 ounces) kidney beans, drained

Cook beef, onion and bell pepper in 10-inch skillet over medium-high heat, stirring occasionally, until beef is brown; drain. Stir in remaining ingredients except beans, breaking up tomatoes.

Heat to boiling; reduce heat to medium-low. Cover and simmer 30 minutes, stirring occasionally. Stir in beans; heat through.

1 Serving: Calories 370 (Calories from Fat 155); Fat 17g (Saturated 7g); Cholesterol 65 mg; Sodium 1580 mg; Carbohydrate 33g (Dietary Fiber 9g); Protein 30g

Marinated Black-Eyed Peas

Chili with Macaroni

6 SERVINGS

1 pound ground beef

1 large onion, chopped (1 cup)

1 medium green bell pepper, chopped (1 cup)

1 can (28 ounces) whole tomatoes, undrained

1 can (15 to 16 ounces) kidney beans, undrained

1 can (8 ounces) tomato sauce

1 cup uncooked elbow macaroni (about 3 ounces)

2 to 4 teaspoons chili powder

1 teaspoon salt

1/8 teaspoon ground red pepper (cayenne)

1/8 teaspoon paprika

Cook beef, onion and bell pepper in 10-inch skillet over medium-high heat, stirring occasionally, until beef is brown; drain. Stir in remaining ingredients, breaking up tomatoes.

Heat to boiling; reduce heat to medium. Cover and simmer 20 to 30 minutes, stirring occasionally, until macaroni is tender.

1 Serving: Calories 330 (Calories from Fat 110); Fat 12g (Saturated 5g); Cholesterol 45 mg; Sodium 1060 mg; Carbohydrate 40g (Dietary Fiber 7g); Protein 23g

White Bean Chili

6 SERVINGS (ABOUT 1 1/2 CUPS EACH)

1/4 cup (1/2 stick) margarine or butter

1 large onion, chopped (1 cup)

1 clove garlic, finely chopped

4 cups cubed cooked chicken

1/4 cup chopped fresh or 1 teaspoon dried basil leaves

3 cups chicken broth

2 tablespoons chopped fresh cilantro or parsley

2 teaspoons chili powder

1/4 teaspoon ground cloves

2 cans (15 to 16 ounces each) great northern beans, undrained

1 medium tomato, chopped (3/4 cup)

Blue or yellow corn tortilla chips

Melt margarine in Dutch oven over medium-high heat. Cook onion and garlic in margarine, stirring occasionally, until onion is tender. Stir in remaining ingredients except tomato and tortilla chips.

Heat to boiling; reduce heat to low. Cover and simmer 1 hour, stirring occasionally. Serve with tomato and tortilla chips.

1 Serving: Calories 541 (Calories from Fat 190); Fat 21g (Saturated 5g); Cholesterol 80 mg; Sodium 1090 mg; Carbohydrate 53g (Dietary Fiber 9g); Protein 44g

Quiche in Green Chile Shell

6 SERVINGS

1/4 pound bulk chorizo or spicy pork sausage

3 cans (4 ounces each) whole green chilies, drained

1 cup shredded Monterey Jack cheese (4 ounces)

1 can (8 ounces) kidney beans, rinsed and drained (about 3/4 to 1 cup)

5 eggs

1/2 cup milk

1/4 teaspoon pepper

Salsa and sour cream, if desired

Heat oven to 350°. Generously grease pie plate, 9 × 1 1/4 inches. Cook sausage in 8-inch skillet over medium-high heat, stirring occasionally, until brown; drain. Cut lengthwise slit in each chile. Open chilies; arrange on bottom and against side of pie plate, forming a shell. Sprinkle with sausage and cheese.

Beat eggs slightly in small bowl. Beat in milk and pepper; pour over sausage, cheese and beans. Bake uncovered about 30 minutes or until knife inserted halfway between center and edge comes out clean. Let stand 10 minutes before cutting. Serve with salsa and sour cream.

1 Serving: Calories 325 (Calories from Fat 225); Fat 25g (Saturated 11g); Cholesterol 230 mg; Sodium 1200 mg; Carbohydrate 5g (Dietary Fiber 0g); Protein 20g

Tortilla-Chicken Soup

5 SERVINGS (ABOUT 1 CUP EACH)

Stale tortillas are used in many ways by Mexican cooks and never wasted. Sliced and fried, they add a distinctive flavor to this chicken soup.

1 tablespoon vegetable oil

4 corn tortillas (5 or 6 inches in diameter), cut into 2 × 1/2-inch strips

1 small onion, chopped (about 1/3 cup)

2 cans (14 1/2 ounces each) ready-to-serve chicken broth

1 can (10 ounces) chopped tomatoes and green chilies, undrained

1 can (6 or 7 ounces) chopped cooked chicken

1 tablespoon lime juice

1 tablespoon chopped fresh cilantro or parsley

Heat 2 teaspoons of the oil in 2-quart saucepan over medium-high heat. Cook tortilla strips in oil 30 to 60 seconds, stirring occasionally, until crisp and light golden brown. Remove from saucepan and drain on paper towels.

Add remaining 1 teaspoon oil and the onion to saucepan. Cook over medium-high heat 3 to 4 minutes, stirring occasionally, until onion is tender. Stir in broth, tomatoes and chicken.

Heat to boiling; reduce heat to low. Simmer uncovered 20 minutes. Stir in lime juice. Serve soup over tortilla strips. Garnish with cilantro.

1 Serving: Calories 160 (Calories from Fat 65); Fat 7g (Saturated 2g); Cholesterol 20 mg; Sodium 820 mg; Carbohydrate 14g (Dietary Fiber 2g); Protein 12g

Zucchíní Soup

5 SERVINGS (ABOUT 1 CUP EACH)

Often gardens yield an abundant amount of summer squash. For variety, you may want to substitute yellow summer squash for all or part of the zucchini.

1 tablespoon margarine or butter

1 small onion, chopped (1/4 cup)

2 cups chicken broth

2 tablespoons canned chopped green chilies

1/2 teaspoon salt

1/8 teaspoon pepper

2 small zucchini, chopped (2 cups)

1 can (8 3/4 ounces) whole kernel corn, drained*

1 cup milk

2 ounces Monterey Jack cheese, cut into 1/4-inch cubes (1/2 cup)

Ground nutmeg

Chopped fresh parsley

Melt margarine in 2-quart saucepan over medium-high heat. Cook onion in margarine, stirring occasionally, until tender. Stir in broth, chilies, salt, pepper, zucchini and corn. Heat to boiling; reduce heat to medium. Cover and simmer about 5 minutes or until zucchini is tender.

Stir in milk; heat just until hot (do not boil). Stir in cheese. Garnish with nutmeg and parsley.

*1 package (10 ounces) frozen whole kernel corn, thawed, can be substituted for the canned corn.

1 Serving: Calories 150 (Calories from Fat 70); Fat 8g (Saturated 4g); Cholesterol 15 mg; Sodium 820 mg; Carbohydrate 13g (Dietary Fiber 2g); Protein 8g

Avocado-Pimíento Swírl Soup

4 SERVINGS (ABOUT 1 CUP EACH)

This soup is elegant in appearance, but quick and easy to prepare in a blender.

1 medium ripe avocado, peeled and cut into fourths

1/2 cup plain yogurt

3 tablespoons lime juice

1/4 teaspoon pepper

2 cans (10 1/2 ounces each) condensed chicken broth

1/2 cup instant mashed potatoes (dry)

1 jar (2 ounces) diced pimientos, drained

1/8 teaspoon ground red pepper (cayenne)

Chopped fresh chives, if desired

Place avocado, yogurt, lime juice, pepper and 1 can of the broth in blender or food processor. Cover and blend on low speed until smooth. Pour soup into storage container; cover and refrigerate. Rinse blender.

Place remaining can of broth, the potatoes, pimientos and red pepper in blender. Cover and blend on low speed until smooth. Pour soup into storage container; cover and refrigerate.

Refrigerate containers of soup up to 24 hours. To serve, divide avocado soup among 4 soup bowls. Pour pimiento soup into pitcher; slowly pour and swirl with knife into avocado soup. Garnish with chives.

1 Serving: Calories 160 (Calories from Fat 80); Fat 9g (Saturated 2g); Cholesterol 2 mg; Sodium 980 mg; Carbohydrate 13g (Dietary Fiber 2g); Protein 9g

Avocado-Pimiento Swirl Soup

4

Poultry, Meat and Seafood

Pine Nut and Green Onion Pilaf (page 52);
Oranges and Cinnamon (page 104); Mexican Chicken (page 67)

Spicy Turkey Burgers

4 SERVINGS

One can (4 ounces) chopped green chilies will be enough to prepare both the burgers and the spread.

1 pound ground turkey

1 small onion, chopped (1/4 cup)

1 clove garlic, chopped

2 to 3 tablespoons canned chopped green chilies

1/8 teaspoon salt

1/8 teaspoon pepper

4 hamburger buns, split

Chile-Cheese Spread (below)

Mix all ingredients except buns and Chile-Cheese Spread. Shape mixture into 4 patties, each about 1/2 inch thick.

Lightly grease cooking surface of grill. Cover and grill patties 4 to 5 inches from medium coals 12 to 15 minutes, turning once, until no longer pink in center. Serve on buns with Chile-Cheese Spread.

Chile-Cheese Spread

1/2 cup shredded Cheddar cheese (2 ounces)

2 tablespoons sour cream

2 tablespoons canned chopped green chilies

Mix all ingredients.

1 Serving: Calories 390 (Calories from Fat 180); Fat 20g (Saturated 8g); Cholesterol 95 mg; Sodium 570 mg; Carbohydrate 24g (Dietary Fiber 1g); Protein 30g

Mexican Chicken Manicotti

4 SERVINGS

The trick to filling manicotti shells without splitting and tearing them is to undercook them by 1 or 2 minutes. Once filled, most recipes are baked and that finishes cooking the manicotti.

8 uncooked manicotti shells

1 package (8 ounces) cream cheese, softened

2 cups shredded Monterey Jack cheese with jalapeño peppers (8 ounces)

2 tablespoons sliced green onions

2 tablespoons chopped fresh cilantro or parsley

1 clove garlic, finely chopped

2 cups cut-up cooked chicken or turkey

1 cup thick-and-chunky salsa

Heat oven to 350°. Cook and drain manicotti shells as directed on package. Mix cream cheese, 1 cup of the Monterey Jack cheese, the onions, cilantro and garlic in medium bowl. Stir in chicken. Fill manicotti shells with chicken mixture.

Arrange filled shells in ungreased rectangular pan, 13 × 9 × 2 inches. Pour salsa over shells. Sprinkle with remaining 1 cup Monterey Jack cheese. Cover and bake 40 to 45 minutes or until filling is hot in center.

1 Serving: Calories 675 (Calories from Fat 385); Fat 43g (Saturated 25g); Cholesterol 175 mg; Sodium 990 mg; Carbohydrate 32g (Dietary Fiber 3g); Protein 43g

Mexican Chicken

6 SERVINGS

1 tablespoon vegetable oil

6 boneless, skinless chicken breast halves

1 medium onion, thinly sliced

2 tablespoons chopped fresh or 1 teaspoon
    dried oregano leaves

2 tablespoons capers

1/2 teaspoon salt

1/4 teaspoon pepper

12 pitted green olives

4 medium tomatoes, chopped (3 cups)

2 medium stalks celery, chopped (1 cup)

2 cloves garlic, finely chopped

2 bay leaves

3 cups sliced mushrooms (8 ounces)

Heat oil in 10-inch skillet over medium-high heat.
Cook chicken and onion in oil, turning once, until
juice of chicken is no longer pink when centers
of thickest pieces are cut. Stir in remaining
ingredients. Heat to boiling; reduce heat to low.
Simmer uncovered 10 to 15 minutes.

Discard bay leaves.

1 Serving: Calories 200 (Calories from Fat 65); Fat 7g
(Saturated 2g); Cholesterol 65 mg; Sodium 450 mg;
Carbohydrate 8g (Dietary Fiber 2g); Protein 28g

Grilled Chicken with Corn-Olive Salsa

6 SERVINGS

Corn-Olive Salsa (page 24)

6 boneless, skinless chicken breast halves

Prepare Corn-Olive Salsa. Cover and grill chicken
4 to 6 inches from medium coals 15 to 20 minutes, turning occasionally, until juice is no longer
pink when centers of thickest pieces are cut. Serve
salsa over chicken.

1 Serving: Calories 230 (Calories from Fat 65); Fat 7g
(Saturated 2g); Cholesterol 65 mg; Sodium 650 mg;
Carbohydrate 16g (Dietary Fiber 2g); Protein 28g

Mexican-Style Citrus-Marinated Chicken

6 SERVINGS

Citrus Marinade (below)

3- to 3 1/2-pound cut-up broiler-fryer chicken

Prepare Citrus Marinade. Place chicken in shallow glass or plastic dish or large, resealable heavy-duty plastic bag. Pour marinade over chicken; turn chicken to coat with marinade. Cover dish or seal bag and refrigerate at least 2 hours but no longer than 24 hours, turning chicken occasionally.

Remove chicken from marinade; reserve marinade. Place chicken, skin sides up, on cooking surface of grill; brush with marinade. Cover and grill 4 to 6 inches from medium coals 15 minutes; turn chicken. Cover and grill 20 to 40 minutes longer, turning and brushing with marinade, until juice of chicken is no longer pink when centers of thickest pieces are cut. Discard any remaining marinade.

Citrus Marinade

1/4 cup orange juice

1/4 cup lime juice

2 tablespoons chopped fresh cilantro or parsley

2 tablespoons olive or vegetable oil

2 teaspoons chili powder

1 teaspoon ground cumin

1/4 teaspoon salt

1/4 teaspoon red pepper sauce

1/2 small onion, chopped

Mix all ingredients.

1 Serving: Calories 240 (Calories from Fat 125); Fat 14g (Saturated 4g); Cholesterol 85 mg; Sodium 130 mg; Carbohydrate 1g (Dietary Fiber 0g); Protein 27g

Southwest Burgers

6 SERVINGS

1 1/2 pounds ground beef

1/2 cup diced Monterey Jack cheese (2 ounces)

1/2 teaspoon pepper

1/4 teaspoon salt

1 can (4 ounces) chopped green chilies, drained

Mix all ingredients. Shape mixture into 6 patties, each about 1/2 inch thick.

Set oven control to broil. Place patties on rack in broiler pan. Broil with tops 3 to 4 inches from heat 10 to 12 minutes, turning once, until no longer pink in center and juice is clear.

1 Serving: Calories 265 (Calories from Fat 170); Fat 19g (Saturated 9g); Cholesterol 75 mg; Sodium 420 mg; Carbohydrate 1g (Dietary Fiber 0g); Protein 23g

Taco Casserole

6 SERVINGS

This casserole is sure to be a big hit. Serve it with a tossed salad with avocado chunks, and cornbread with honey and butter.

1 pound ground beef

1 can (15 ounces) chili beans

1 can (8 ounces) tomato sauce

2 tablespoons taco sauce, picante sauce or salsa

2 to 4 teaspoons chili powder

1 teaspoon garlic powder

2 cups coarsely broken tortilla chips

1 cup sour cream

1/2 cup sliced green onions (5 medium)

1 medium tomato, chopped (3/4 cup)

1 cup shredded Cheddar or Monterey Jack cheese (4 ounces)

Shredded lettuce and taco sauce, if desired

Heat oven to 350°. Cook beef in 10-inch skillet over medium-high heat, stirring occasionally, until brown; drain. Stir in beans, tomato sauce, 2 tablespoons taco sauce, the chili powder and garlic powder. Heat to boiling, stirring occasionally.

Place tortilla chips in ungreased 2-quart casserole. Top with beef mixture. Spread with sour cream. Sprinkle with onions, tomato and cheese.

Bake uncovered 20 to 30 minutes or until hot and bubbly. Arrange additional tortilla chips around edge of casserole if desired. Serve with lettuce and taco sauce.

1 Serving: Calories 390 (Calories from Fat 235); Fat 26g (Saturated 13g); Cholesterol 85 mg; Sodium 740 mg; Carbohydrate 20g (Dietary Fiber 4g); Protein 23g

FESTIVE FOOD TOUCHES

Tortilla Tie-ups: Add a festive look to flour tortillas by tying them with green onion tops. To soften green onion tops making them easier to work with, place in boiling water a few seconds and then into iced water; drain on paper towels. Roll up tortillas, and tie with green onion tops.

Fancy Tortilla Cut-ups: Add zigzag edges to tortilla strips and wedges by cutting with a crimped pastry wheel, pinking shears or crinkle cutter. Or, use small cookie cutters to create fun shapes.

Easy Platter or Plate Garnish: Brush rim of platter or individual serving plates with water; sprinkle with chopped fresh cilantro or parsley. Sprinkle with chili powder or pepper too, if desired.

Taco Tossed Salad

6 SERVINGS

Love taco salad but not all of the fat and calories? No problem! Lighten it by using ground turkey breast in place of ground beef, coarsely crushed baked tortilla chips versus corn chips, and reduced-fat cheese and salad dressing.

1 pound ground beef

1/2 cup taco or picante sauce

6 cups torn lettuce

1 medium green bell pepper, cut into strips

2 medium tomatoes, cut into wedges

1/2 cup pitted ripe olives, drained

1 cup corn chips

1 cup shredded Cheddar cheese (4 ounces)

Salsa or picante sauce, if desired

Cook beef in 10-inch skillet over medium-high heat, stirring occasionally, until brown; drain. Stir in taco sauce; heat through.

Toss lettuce, bell pepper, tomatoes, olives and corn chips in large bowl. Spoon hot beef mixture over lettuce mixture; toss. Sprinkle with cheese. Serve immediately with salsa.

1 Serving: Calories 285 (Calories from Fat 180); Fat 20g (Saturated 9g); Cholesterol 65 mg; Sodium 420 mg; Carbohydrate 8g (Dietary Fiber 2g); Protein 20g

Mexican Lasagne

8 SERVINGS

1 package (8 ounces) lasagne noodles

1 pound ground beef

1 medium onion, chopped (1/2 cup)

1/4 cup chopped fresh cilantro or parsley

1 teaspoon chili powder

1 container (15 ounces) low-fat ricotta cheese

1 jar (24 ounces) salsa (about 3 cups)

1 cup shredded Monterey Jack cheese (4 ounces)

Heat oven to 375°. Cook and drain noodles as directed on package. Cook beef, onion, cilantro and chili powder in 10-inch skillet over medium-high heat, stirring occasionally, until beef is brown; drain.

Place 5 of the noodles in bottom of ungreased rectangular pan, 13 × 9 × 2 inches. Layer with 1 1/2 cups of the beef mixture, 1 cup of the ricotta cheese and 1 1/4 cups of the salsa. Repeat with remaining noodles, beef mixture, ricotta cheese and salsa. Sprinkle with Monterey Jack cheese.

Bake uncovered 35 to 40 minutes or until hot. Let stand 10 minutes before cutting.

1 Serving: Calories 365 (Calories from Fat 170); Fat 19g (Saturated 9g); Cholesterol 85 mg; Sodium 690 mg; Carbohydrate 28g (Dietary Fiber 4g); Protein 24g

Taco Tossed Salad

Herbed Flank Steak

8 SERVINGS

1/2 cup lime juice

1/4 cup chopped fresh or 2 tablespoons dried oregano leaves

2 tablespoons olive or vegetable oil

1/2 teaspoon salt

1/2 teaspoon pepper

4 cloves garlic, crushed

2 beef flank steaks (1 to 1 1/2 pounds each)

Mix all ingredients except beef in shallow glass or plastic dish or large, resealable heavy-duty plastic bag. Add beef; turn to coat with marinade. Cover dish or seal bag and refrigerate 15 to 30 minutes, turning beef once.

Remove beef from marinade; discard marinade. Cover and grill beef 4 to 5 inches from medium coals 10 to 15 minutes for medium doneness, turning once. Cut beef diagonally across grain into thin slices.

1 Serving: Calories 240 (Calories from Fat 115); Fat 13g (Saturated 4g); Cholesterol 75 mg; Sodium 200 mg; Carbohydrate 2g (Dietary Fiber 0g); Protein 29g

Mexican Steak

4 SERVINGS

Sour cream, cool and smooth, is spooned onto simmered steak strips for a pleasant flavor contrast.

1 pound beef tenderloin or boneless top loin steak, about 1/2 inch thick

1 tablespoon vegetable oil

1 medium onion, chopped (1/2 cup)

1 can (15 ounces) chunky Mexican-style tomato sauce

1 teaspoon chili powder

1 teaspoon ground cumin

1/3 cup sour cream

1 tablespoon chopped fresh parsley or cilantro

Cut beef across grain into strips, each 1 1/2 × 1/2 inch. (Beef is easier to cut if partially frozen, about 1 1/2 hours.) Heat oil in 10-inch skillet over medium-high heat. Cook beef and onion in oil, stirring occasionally, until beef is brown. Stir in tomato sauce, chili powder and cumin.

Heat to boiling; reduce heat to low. Cover and simmer about 15 minutes or until beef is tender. Top with sour cream. Sprinkle with parsley.

1 Serving: Calories 290 (Calories from Fat 160); Fat 18g (Saturated 6g); Cholesterol 70 mg; Sodium 430 mg; Carbohydrate 11g (Dietary Fiber 2g); Protein 23g

Mexican Steak; Tex-Mex Coleslaw (page 96)

Cinco de Mayo Celebration

Cinco de Mayo is a national holiday in Mexico recalling the May 5th Battle of Puebla fought in 1862. Although Mexico's troops were outnumbered by the French three to one, they won the battle. Today the victory is remembered with parades, festivals, speeches and, of course, bountiful and delicious food! Foods served for Cinco de Mayo vary from region to region and home to home as no particular food ultimately defines this holiday.

Celebrate Mexico's independence with a casual, festive and fun atmosphere and a meal of foods from south of the border. To help you set the tone for this fiesta, we offer a complete menu and tips for decorations, party favors and music.

CINCO DE MAYO MENU

Mexican Pinwheels (page 12)
Nifty Nachos (page 10)
Southwest Burgers (page 68)
Mexican Flag Salad (page 90)
Easy Margarita Pie (page 103)
Sangria (page 115)

Festive Touches

Decorations, Party Favors and Music

- Dress up tabletops with colorful ponchos, serapes or blankets instead of tablecloths.
- Check paper and party decorating stores for inexpensive theme decorations as well as colorful paper or plastic plates, place mats, napkins, silverware and cups.
- For an outdoor party, string chile pepper lights and burn citronella candles.
- Accent tables and counters with small Mexican flags.
- Create a centerpiece by filling a large bowl or basket with an assortment of any of the following typically Mexican ingredients: bell peppers, onions, avocados, oranges, limes, tomatoes, squash, gourds or Indian corn.
- Place a small cactus plant (real or artificial) at each place setting for a party favor.
- Place cookie cutters in the shape of cactus or coyotes at each place setting and tie a colorful bow around each.
- Play mariachi or marimba music. If you don't have this type of music, you may be able to find it in your local library.

Food Accents

- Line a sombrero with a colorful paper napkin and fill with tortilla chips.
- Serve your favorite dip in a colorful bell pepper. Cut a large bell pepper lengthwise in half and remove the seeds and membranes. Fill with dip.
- Line serving platters or baskets with dried corn husks.

Caramelized Carnitas

4 SERVINGS

The slightly sweet flavor of this pork dish is excellent served with fresh sweet potatoes that have been baked or mashed.

1 1/2-pound pork boneless shoulder, cut into 1-inch cubes

2 tablespoons packed brown sugar

1 tablespoon tequila or orange juice

1 tablespoon molasses

1/2 teaspoon salt

1/4 teaspoon pepper

2 cloves garlic, finely chopped

1/3 cup water

1 green onion, sliced

Place pork in single layer in 10-inch skillet. Top with remaining ingredients except onion. Heat to boiling; reduce heat to low.

Simmer uncovered about 35 minutes, stirring occasionally, until water has evaporated and pork is slightly caramelized. Sprinkle with onion.

1 Serving: Calories 270 (Calories from Fat 125); Fat 14g (Saturated 5g); Cholesterol 75 mg; Sodium 320 mg; Carbohydrate 11g (Dietary Fiber 0g); Protein 25g

Spicy Pork Roast

6 SERVINGS

1/4 cup sugar

1 teaspoon chili powder

1 teaspoon dried oregano leaves

1/2 teaspoon pepper

2-pound pork boneless loin roast

Mix sugar, chili powder, oregano and pepper; rub into pork. Cover and refrigerate 30 minutes.

Heat oven to 325°. Place pork, fat side up, on rack in shallow roasting pan. Insert meat thermometer so tip is in thickest part of pork and does not rest in fat. Roast uncovered about 2 hours or until thermometer reads 160°.

1 Serving: Calories 215 (Calories from Fat 80); Fat 9g (Saturated 3g); Cholesterol 70 mg; Sodium 45 mg; Carbohydrate 9g (Dietary Fiber 0g); Protein 24g

Herbed Flank Steak (page 72);
Southwest Vegetable Sauté (page 86)

Tex-Mex Pizza

8 SLICES

1/4 pound bulk chorizo or spicy pork sausage

1 1/2 cups shredded Monterey Jack cheese (6 ounces)

1 Italian bread shell or purchased pizza crust (12 inches in diameter)

1 jar (8 ounces) salsa (about 1 cup)

1 small bell pepper, chopped (1/2 cup)

1/2 cup canned black beans, rinsed and drained, or 1 can (2 1/4 ounces) sliced ripe olives, drained

Heat oven to 450°. Cook sausage in 8-inch skillet over medium-high heat, stirring occasionally, until brown; drain.

Sprinkle 1 cup of the cheese over bread shell. Top with salsa, sausage, bell pepper and beans. Sprinkle with remaining cheese.

Place on ungreased cookie sheet. Bake 8 to 10 minutes or until pizza is hot and cheese is melted.

1 Serving: Calories 275 (Calories from Fat 135); Fat 15g (Saturated 7g); Cholesterol 35 mg; Sodium 680 mg; Carbohydrate 26g (Dietary Fiber 3g); Protein 12g

Ranch-Style Eggs

6 SERVINGS

The Mexican name for this famous breakfast specialty is huevos rancheros. *Fresh fruit would make a refreshing accompaniment to these zesty fried eggs.*

1/2 pound bulk pork sausage

Vegetable oil

6 corn tortillas (5 or 6 inches in diameter)

1 1/4 cups picante sauce or salsa, heated

6 fried eggs

1 1/2 cups shredded Cheddar or Monterey Jack cheese (6 ounces)

Cook sausage in 8-inch skillet over medium-high heat, stirring occasionally, until brown; drain. Heat 1/8 inch oil in 8-inch skillet over medium heat. Cook tortillas, 1 at a time, in hot oil until crisp, about 1 minute. Drain on paper towels.

Spread 1 tablespoon of the picante sauce over each tortilla to soften. Place 1 egg on each tortilla. Top each egg with 1 scant tablespoon of the sauce, 1/4 cup of the sausage, another tablespoon of the sauce and 1/4 cup of the cheese.

1 Serving: Calories 355 (Calories from Fat 225); Fat 25g (Saturated 11g); Cholesterol 260 mg; Sodium 990 mg; Carbohydrate 16g (Dietary Fiber 2g); Protein 19g

Tex-Mex Pizza

Mexican-Style Fish Grilled in Foil

6 SERVINGS

1 1/2 pounds halibut, cod or red snapper fillets, 1/2 to 3/4 inch thick

1/4 cup sliced pimiento-stuffed olives

2 teaspoons capers

3 green onions, thinly sliced

1 medium tomato, seeded and coarsely chopped (3/4 cup)

1 clove garlic, finely chopped

2 tablespoons lemon juice

1/4 teaspoon salt

1/8 teaspoon pepper

Lemon wedges

If fish fillets are large, cut into 6 serving pieces. Place each piece fish on 12-inch square of heavy-duty aluminum foil. Mix olives, capers, onions, tomato and garlic; spoon over fish. Drizzle with lemon juice. Sprinkle with salt and pepper. Wrap foil securely.

Cover and grill foil packets, seam sides up, 4 to 6 inches from medium coals 15 to 20 minutes, turning once, until fish flakes easily with fork. Serve with lemon wedges.

1 Serving: Calories 100 (Calories from Fat 20); Fat 2g (Saturated 1g); Cholesterol 50 mg; Sodium 320 mg; Carbohydrate 2g (Dietary Fiber 0g); Protein 18g

Grilled Fish with Melon-Jicama Salsa

6 SERVINGS

Melon-Jicama Salsa (page 22)

1 1/2 pounds swordfish, tuna or marlin steaks, 3/4 to 1 inch thick

3 tablespoons olive or vegetable oil

1 tablespoon lime juice

1/4 teaspoon salt

1/8 teaspoon crushed red pepper

Lime wedges, if desired

Prepare Melon-Jicama Salsa. If fish steaks are large, cut into 6 serving pieces. Mix oil, lime juice, salt and red pepper in shallow glass or plastic dish or large, resealable heavy-duty plastic bag. Add fish; turn to coat with marinade. Cover dish or seal bag and refrigerate 30 minutes.

Remove fish from marinade; reserve marinade. Cover and grill fish 5 to 6 inches from medium coals 10 minutes, brushing 2 or 3 times with marinade and turning once, until fish flakes easily with fork. Discard any remaining marinade. Serve fish with salsa. Garnish with lime wedges.

1 Serving: Calories 210 (Calories from Fat 110); Fat 12g (Saturated 3g); Cholesterol 55 mg; Sodium 150 mg; Carbohydrate 7g (Dietary Fiber 0g); Protein 18g

Grilled Fish with Melon-Jicama Salsa

5

Vegetables and Salads

Rio Grande Melon Salad (page 94); Zesty Potato Salad (page 96);
Green Beans Olé (page 85)

Potatoes con Queso

4 SERVINGS

The "heat" in this dish can be varied by the type of salsa used—mild, medium or hot.

3 medium potatoes (1 pound), peeled and cut into 1-inch pieces

4 ounces process cheese loaf, diced (3/4 cup)

1/2 cup salsa

1 tablespoon chopped fresh cilantro or parsley

Heat 1 inch water to boiling in 2-quart saucepan. Add potatoes. Cover and heat to boiling; reduce heat to medium-low. Cook 20 to 25 minutes or until tender; drain.

Return potatoes to saucepan. Add cheese and salsa. Cover and let stand 2 minutes. Uncover and gently stir until cheese is melted. Garnish with cilantro.

1 Serving: Calories 190 (Calories from Fat 80); Fat 9g (Saturated 6g); Cholesterol 25 mg; Sodium 620 mg; Carbohydrate 21g (Dietary Fiber 2g); Protein 8g

Red Onion-Topped Potatoes

6 SERVINGS

3 large baking potatoes (1 1/2 pounds)

Salt and pepper to taste

1 cup grated Parmesan or Romano cheese

3/4 cup finely chopped red onion

1 tablespoon chopped fresh cilantro or parsley

1 clove garlic, finely chopped

Heat oven to 375°. Bake potatoes about 1 hour or until tender

Cut potatoes lengthwise in half. Cut surface of potatoes in crisscross pattern 1/2 inch deep, being careful not to cut through skin. Sprinkle with salt and pepper.

Mix remaining ingredients; divide among potatoes. Press onion mixture down into crisscross pattern and on top of each potato. Bake about 5 minutes or until hot.

1 Serving: Calories 130 (Calories from Fat 35); Fat 4g (Saturated 3g); Cholesterol 10 mg; Sodium 520 mg; Carbohydrate 18g (Dietary Fiber 1g); Protein 7g

Green Beans Olé

4 SERVINGS

1 pound green beans, cut up

4 slices bacon, cut up

1 medium onion, chopped (1/2 cup)

1 medium tomato, chopped (3/4 cup)

1 clove garlic, finely chopped

**1 teaspoon chopped fresh or 1/2 teaspoon
     dried oregano leaves**

1/2 teaspoon salt

Dash of pepper

2 tablespoons lemon or lime juice

Place beans in 1 inch water in 2-quart saucepan. Heat to boiling; reduce heat to low. Simmer uncovered 10 to 15 minutes or until crisp-tender; drain. Immediately rinse with cold water; drain.

Cook bacon in 10-inch skillet over medium-high heat until crisp; drain all but 1 tablespoon fat from skillet. Drain bacon on paper towels. Cook onion in bacon fat over medium heat, stirring occasionally, until tender.

Stir in tomato, garlic, oregano, salt and pepper. Simmer uncovered 5 minutes. Stir in beans; heat through. Drizzle with lemon juice. Garnish with bacon

1 Serving: Calories 70 (Calories from Fat 25); Fat 3g (Saturated 1g); Cholesterol 5 mg; Sodium 390 mg; Carbohydrate 11g (Dietary Fiber 4g); Protein 4g

---

JICAMA

The flesh of the jicama root is often compared to a water chestnut, both for flavor and crunch. Even when cooked, the ivory flesh remains crisp. Jicama is related to the sharp-tasting turnip but is so mild in flavor that when eaten raw, it is often sprinkled with lemon or lime juice and chili powder. After the brown fibrous skin has been peeled away, jicama flesh does not discolor. It can range in size from one to six pounds.

Selection and Storage

Look for firm, evenly shaped jicama that is free from mold and blemishes. Smaller roots will be more moist and sweet.

Whole jicama can be stored in a cool (50°), dark and dry place for up to three weeks. Cut jicama should be stored in the refrigerator tightly covered or wrapped for up to one week.

Serving Ideas

- For a low-fat appetizer, dip slices of jicama into lime juice and dip into chili powder or seasoned salt.

- Shred and use in coleslaw.

- Add diced or shredded jicama to tossed salads.

- Add julienne strips to stir-fry recipes.

- Use slices as dippers for guacamole, salsa or spicy peanut sauce.

- Add diced jicama to Waldorf, carrot-raisin or fruit salad mixtures.

Southwest Vegetable Sauté

8 SERVINGS

If chayote squash isn't available in your area, substitute zucchini or yellow summer squash.

1/4 cup (1/2 stick) margarine or butter

1 medium onion, finely chopped (1/2 cup)

2 cloves garlic, finely chopped

4 very small pattypan squash (about 4 ounces each), cut in half

2 small zucchini, cut into 1/4-inch strips

2 small yellow summer squash, cut into 1/4-inch slices

1 medium chayote, peeled and cut into 1/2-inch cubes

1 small red bell pepper, cut into thin rings

1 small yellow bell pepper, cut into thin rings

1/2 teaspoon salt

1/4 teaspoon ground red pepper (cayenne)

Margarine or butter, melted, and grated lime peel, if desired

Melt 1/4 cup margarine in 12-inch skillet over medium-high heat. Cook onion and garlic in margarine, stirring occasionally, until onion is tender.

Stir in remaining ingredients except melted margarine. Cook over medium-high heat, stirring occasionally, until vegetables are crisp-tender. Drizzle with melted margarine, and sprinkle with lime peel.

1 Serving: Calories 80 (Calories from Fat 55); Fat 6g (Saturated 1g); Cholesterol 0 mg; Sodium 200 mg; Carbohydrate 7g (Dietary Fiber 2g); Protein 1g

Cinnamon Squash Rings

6 SERVINGS

2 tablespoons packed brown sugar

2 tablespoons milk

1 egg

3/4 cup soft bread crumbs (about 2 1/2 slices bread)

1/4 cup cornmeal

2 teaspoons ground cinnamon

1 large acorn squash (1 1/2 pounds), cut crosswise into 1/2-inch slices and seeded

1/3 cup margarine or butter, melted

Heat oven to 400°. Mix brown sugar, milk and egg. Mix bread crumbs, cornmeal and cinnamon. Dip squash slices into egg mixture, then coat with bread crumb mixture; repeat.

Place in ungreased rectangular pan, $13 \times 9 \times 2$ inches. Drizzle with margarine. Bake uncovered 30 to 35 minutes or until squash is tender.

1 Serving: Calories 190 (Calories from Fat 110); Fat 12g (Saturated 3g); Cholesterol 35 mg; Sodium 190 mg; Carbohydrate 21g (Dietary Fiber 3g); Protein 3g

Cinnamon Squash Rings

Zucchini and Hominy

6 SERVINGS

2 tablespoons vegetable oil

2 tablespoons margarine or butter

1 small onion, chopped (1/4 cup)

3 medium zucchini, cut into 1/2-inch pieces

2 medium tomatoes, chopped (1 1/2 cups)

1 can (14 1/2 ounces) hominy, drained

1 tablespoon chili powder

2 tablespoons lime juice

1 teaspoon salt

Dash of pepper

Heat oil and margarine in 10-inch skillet over medium-high heat. Cook onion in oil mixture, stirring occasionally, until tender. Stir in remaining ingredients.

Cook uncovered over medium-high heat 5 to 10 minutes, stirring occasionally, until zucchini is tender.

1 Serving: Calories 160 (Calories from Fat 90); Fat 10g (Saturated 2g); Cholesterol 0 mg; Sodium 590 mg; Carbohydrate 18g (Dietary Fiber 4g); Protein 3g

Eggplant Acapulco

8 SERVINGS

Here's an out-of-the-ordinary eggplant dish that is great for a buffet supper.

1 small eggplant (1 pound), peeled and cut into 1/2-inch cubes

1 1/2 cups coarsely crushed corn chips (3 ounces)

1 cup shredded Cheddar cheese (4 ounces)

1 can (15 ounces) chunky Mexican-style tomato sauce

Heat oven to 350°. Grease square baking dish, 8 × 8 × 2 inches. Heat 1/2 inch water to boiling in 2-quart saucepan. Add eggplant. Cover and heat to boiling; reduce heat to medium-high. Cook 5 minutes; drain.

Mix corn chips and cheese. Spread half of the eggplant in baking dish; spoon half of the tomato sauce over eggplant. Sprinkle with half of the corn chip mixture. Repeat with remaining eggplant, tomato sauce and corn chip mixture. Bake uncovered about 30 minutes or until bubbly around edges.

1 Serving: Calories 140 (Calories from Fat 80); Fat 9g (Saturated 4g); Cholesterol 15 mg; Sodium 460 mg; Carbohydrate 12g (Dietary Fiber 2g); Protein 5g

Mexican Succotash

6 SERVINGS

This colorful vegetable combination would taste great with grilled burgers or chicken.

1 tablespoon vegetable oil

1 medium onion, chopped (1/2 cup)

3 medium zucchini, cut into 1/2-inch slices

1 1/2 cups frozen whole kernel corn

1 tablespoon chopped fresh or 1 teaspoon dried oregano leaves

1/2 teaspoon salt

Dash of pepper

1 can (28 ounces) whole tomatoes, undrained

Heat oil in 10-inch skillet over medium-high heat. Cook onion in oil, stirring occasionally, until tender. Stir in zucchini. Cook 1 minute, stirring occasionally. Stir in remaining ingredients, breaking up tomatoes.

Heat to boiling; reduce heat to low. Cover and simmer 7 to 10 minutes or until zucchini is tender.

1 Serving: Calories 100 (Calories from Fat 25); Fat 3g (Saturated 1g); Cholesterol 0 mg; Sodium 400 mg; Carbohydrate 18g (Dietary Fiber 4g); Protein 4g

Jicama-Citrus Salad with Sangria Dressing

8 SERVINGS

3 large oranges, peeled and sectioned

2 red grapefruit, peeled and sectioned

1 medium jicama (about 1 1/2 pounds), peeled and cut into 1/2-inch cubes

Sangria Dressing (below)

Arrange oranges, grapefruit and jicama on 8 salad plates, or mix together in large bowl. Serve with Sangria Dressing.

Sangria Dressing

1/4 cup vegetable oil

1/4 cup dry red wine or apple juice

2 tablespoons honey

2 tablespoons orange juice

Mix all ingredients.

1 Serving: Calories 160 (Calories from Fat 65); Fat 7g (Saturated 1g); Cholesterol 0 mg; Sodium 5 mg; Carbohydrate 26g (Dietary Fiber 4g); Protein 2g

Mexican Flag Salad

6 TO 8 SERVINGS

1 pound whole green beans

1 small jicama (about 1 pound), peeled and cut into 1/4-inch strips (2 cups)

2 medium red bell peppers, cut into 1/4-inch strips

1 bottle (8 ounces) Italian dressing

1 tablespoon lime juice

Lettuce leaves

6 to 8 pitted ripe olives, finely chopped

Place beans in 1 inch water in 2-quart saucepan. Heat to boiling; reduce heat to low. Simmer uncovered 10 to 15 minutes or until crisp-tender; drain. Immediately rinse with cold water; drain.

Place beans, jicama and bell peppers in separate bowls. Mix dressing and lime juice. Pour 1/4 cup dressing mixture over each vegetable. Cover and refrigerate at least 1 hour.

Line large rectangular platter with lettuce leaves. Arrange beans on left end of platter, jicama in the middle and peppers on the right end of platter to form Mexican flag design. Place olives in center of rectangle formed by jicama.

1 Serving: Calories 225 (Calories from Fat 170); Fat 19g (Saturated 3g); Cholesterol 0 mg; Sodium 350 mg; Carbohydrate 15g (Dietary Fiber 4g); Protein 2g

ABOUT MEXICAN FLAG SALAD

The three-color design of the Mexican flag was approved in 1821, when the country became independent from Spain. The green symbolizes the lofty hopes and independence of the new republic; the white stands for religion and the purity of its endeavors; and the red represents union and the valor displayed in pursuit of these noble goals. In the center of the white panel is the coat of arms.

Mexican Flag Salad represents these colors with green, white and red vegetables and the chopped ripe olives simulate the black eagle on the flag.

Mexicali Pasta Salad

6 SERVINGS

3 cups uncooked tricolor rotini (spiral) pasta (about 8 ounces)

6 small tomatillos or green tomatoes, each cut into 8 wedges

1/2 jalapeño chile, seeded and finely chopped

1 can (20 ounces) pineapple chunks in juice, drained and 2 tablespoons juice reserved

1 tablespoon chopped fresh cilantro or parsley

2 tablespoons vegetable oil

1/2 teaspoon grated lime peel

1/4 teaspoon salt

Cook and drain pasta as directed on package. Rinse with cold water; drain. Mix pasta, tomatillos, chile and pineapple in large glass or plastic bowl.

Mix reserved pineapple juice and the remaining ingredients. Pour over pasta mixture; toss. Cover and refrigerate about 2 hours to blend flavors.

1 Serving: Calories 255 (Calories from Fat 55); Fat 6g (Saturated 1g); Cholesterol 0 mg; Sodium 100 mg; Carbohydrate 47g (Dietary Fiber 3g); Protein 6g

Mexican Turkey and Broccoli Salad

4 SERVINGS

2 cups cut-up cooked smoked turkey

2 cups cooked rotelle or rotini (spiral) pasta

2 cups purchased broccoli slaw

1 small red bell pepper, chopped (1/2 cup)

1 cup ranch dressing with tomato, onion and spicy peppers

Mix all ingredients. Cover and refrigerate at least 1 hour to blend flavors.

1 Serving: Calories 590 (Calories from Fat 245); Fat 27g (Saturated 5g); Cholesterol 80 mg; Sodium 560 mg; Carbohydrate 58g (Dietary Fiber 3g); Protein 32g

Mexican Turkey and Broccoli Salad

Río Grande Melon Salad

6 SERVINGS

2 cups watermelon balls

2 mangoes or papayas, peeled, seeded and sliced

1/2 honeydew melon, peeled, seeded and thinly sliced

3/4 cup seedless red grapes

Lettuce leaves

Honey-Lime Dressing (below)

Arrange fruits on lettuce leaves. Drizzle with Honey-Lime Dressing.

Honey-Lime Dressing

1/4 cup vegetable oil

1/4 teaspoon grated lime peel

2 tablespoons lime juice

1 tablespoon honey

Shake all ingredients in tightly covered container.

1 Serving: Calories 215 (Calories from Fat 90); Fat 10g (Saturated 2g); Cholesterol 0 mg; Sodium 15 mg; Carbohydrate 33g (Dietary Fiber 3g); Protein 1g

Chicken and Orange Salad

6 SERVINGS

1 package (16 ounces) frozen cauliflower, carrots and asparagus, thawed and drained

2 cups cut-up cooked chicken

2/3 cup mayonnaise or salad dressing

1/4 cup finely chopped cilantro or parsley

2 tablespoons chopped green onions

3 tablespoons orange juice

1/2 teaspoon ground cinnamon

1/4 teaspoon salt

1/4 teaspoon freshly ground pepper

Lettuce leaves

2 oranges, peeled and sectioned

1 avocado, cut into wedges

Mix vegetables and remaining ingredients except lettuce, oranges and avocado in glass or plastic bowl. Cover and refrigerate at least 1 hour to blend flavors. Just before serving, add oranges. Toss gently.

Serve salad on lettuce leaves. Garnish with oranges and avocado.

1 Serving: Calories 435 (Calories from Fat 335); Fat 37g (Saturated 6g); Cholesterol 60 mg; Sodium 360 mg; Carbohydrate 14g (Dietary Fiber 4g); Protein 16g

Chicken and Orange Salad

Tex-Mex Coleslaw

8 SERVINGS

This extra-crunchy coleslaw has a spicy salsa kick.

1/3 cup picante sauce

1 tablespoon sugar

3 tablespoons white vinegar

2 tablespoons vegetable oil

4 cups coarsely shredded cabbage (1 pound)

2 cups coarsely shredded jicama (3/4 pound)

2 medium carrots, coarsely shredded (1 cup)

4 green onions, thinly sliced

Mix picante sauce, sugar, vinegar and oil in large glass or plastic bowl. Add remaining ingredients; toss. Cover and refrigerate at least 2 hours but no longer than 24 hours.

1 Serving: Calories 70 (Calories from Fat 35); Fat 4g (Saturated 1g); Cholesterol 0 mg; Sodium 85 mg; Carbohydrate 10g (Dietary Fiber 2g); Protein 1g

Zesty Potato Salad

6 SERVINGS

The "heat" in green chilies varies a great deal. Taste them before adding to your favorite recipe and adjust accordingly.

10 to 12 new potatoes (1 1/2 pounds)

3/4 cup mayonnaise or salad dressing

2 tablespoons canned chopped green chilies

1 tablespoon lemon juice

1/2 teaspoon ground cumin

1/2 teaspoon salt

2 medium stalks celery, sliced (1 cup)

1 small red bell pepper, chopped (1/2 cup)

1/4 cup chopped ripe olives

Heat 1 inch water to boiling in 2-quart saucepan. Add potatoes. Cover and heat to boiling; reduce heat to medium-low. Cook 20 to 25 minutes or until tender; drain and cool. Cut potatoes into 2-inch cubes.

Mix mayonnaise, chilies, lemon juice, cumin and salt in large glass or plastic bowl. Add potatoes and remaining ingredients; toss. Cover and refrigerate at least 2 hours to blend flavors.

1 Serving: Calories 365 (Calories from Fat 205); Fat 23g (Saturated 4g); Cholesterol 15 mg; Sodium 440 mg; Carbohydrate 39g (Dietary Fiber 3g); Protein 4g

ALL ABOUT AVOCADOS

Originating from the tropics, this luscious, buttery-fleshed fruit has a rich, slightly nutty flavor. Avocados were introduced into Florida in the mid-1800s and were once considered exotic. Currently, 85 percent of all avocados grown in the United States come from California and the rest from Florida. Although available all year, avocados are actually seasonal, with different varieties ripening at different times. Below we describe the types most widely available.

Types of Avocados

Haas: Available spring through late fall. It is oval-shaped with pebbly skin changing from green to black as it ripens. The flesh is rich and buttery. It is more flavorful than the other varieties due to a higher fat content.

Fuerte: Available through the winter months. It is pear-shaped with smooth, green skin that remains green upon ripening. It is more mildly flavored than Haas.

Bacon and Zutano: Available fall and winter. The oval-shaped Bacon and pear-shaped Zutano are smaller than Haas and Fuerte types. Both have smooth, green skin that remains green upon ripening. The flesh is quite mild and more watery in texture.

Selection and Storage

Avocados are ripe when they yield to gentle pressure. Additionally, the skin of the Haas variety turns dark green to black when ripe. Avoid fruit that has blemishes, sunken spots or is soft.

Ripen hard avocados by placing them in a loosely closed paper bag and allowing them to stand at room temperature two to four days. Once ripened, store them in the refrigerator for up to two days.

Cut avocados turn brown very quickly. To help prevent browning, brush cut surfaces with lemon or lime juice or add lemon or lime juice to mashed avocado mixtures. It is a myth that burying the avocado pit in the guacamole will prevent browning.

6

Desserts and Beverages

Flan (page 106)

Frozen Cinnamon-Chocolate Dessert

8 SERVINGS

1 cup chocolate wafer cookie crumbs (about 20 cookies)

1/4 cup (1/2 stick) margarine or butter, melted

1 quart cinnamon, vanilla or chocolate ice cream, softened

Cinnamon-Chocolate Sauce (right)

Mix cookie crumbs and margarine. Press in bottom of ungreased springform pan, 8 × 2 inches. Freeze 10 minutes.

Spoon ice cream onto crumb crust; smooth top. Cover and freeze about 2 hours or until firm. Run metal spatula along side of pan to loosen; remove side of pan. Serve dessert with Cinnamon-Chocolate Sauce. Freeze any remaining dessert.

Cinnamon-Chocolate Sauce

1/2 cup whipping (heavy) cream

1/4 cup sugar

1 ounce unsweetened chocolate

1/2 teaspoon ground cinnamon

Heat whipping cream, sugar and chocolate to boiling in 1-quart saucepan over medium heat, stirring constantly. Boil and stir about 30 seconds or until chocolate is melted; remove from heat. Stir in cinnamon. Serve warm or cool.

1 Serving: Calories 345 (Calories from Fat 200); Fat 22g (Saturated 11g); Cholesterol 45 mg; Sodium 210 mg; Carbohydrate 34g (Dietary Fiber 1g); Protein 4g

Mexican Sundaes

4 SERVINGS

1 tablespoon sugar

2 tablespoons cinnamon-flavored international instant coffee mix

1 tablespoon cocoa

1 teaspoon cornstarch

1 can (5 ounces) evaporated milk

1 pint coffee ice cream

Mix sugar, coffee mix, cocoa and cornstarch in 1-quart saucepan. Gradually stir in milk. Heat over medium heat, stirring constantly, until mixture thickens and boils. Boil and stir 1 minute; remove from heat. Cool slightly.

Press plastic wrap or waxed paper onto surface of sauce. Let stand about 30 minutes. Spoon ice cream into dessert dishes. Top with warm sauce.

1 Serving: Calories 230 (Calories from Fat 100); Fat 11g (Saturated 7g); Cholesterol 40 mg; Sodium 130 mg; Carbohydrate 28g (Dietary Fiber 0g); Protein 5g

Limeade Sorbet

4 SERVINGS

This refreshing dessert can also be made in an ice-cream freezer. Blend all the ingredients as directed and pour into the ice-cream freezer. Freeze according to manufacturer's directions.

1 1/2 cups cold water

1 cup frozen limeade concentrate

3 tablespoons honey

Lime slices and fresh raspberries, if desired

Place water, limeade concentrate and honey in blender or food processor. Cover and blend until smooth. Pour mixture into square baking dish, 8 × 8 × 2 inches.

Cover and freeze about 2 to 4 hours, stirring several times to keep mixture smooth, until firm. Spoon into dessert dishes. Garnish with lime slices and raspberries.

1 Serving: Calories 155 (Calories from Fat 0); Fat 0g (Saturated 0g); Cholesterol 0 mg; Sodium 10 mg; Carbohydrate 39g (Dietary Fiber 0g); Protein 0g

Cinnamon "Fried" Ice Cream

6 SERVINGS

Did we say fried? No way! This crunchy broiled Mexican ice cream is just as delicious as the high-fat, deep-fat fried ice cream.

3 cups cinnamon toast-flavored cereal, crushed

6 scoops (1/2 cup each) vanilla ice cream

Place cereal in shallow pan. Quickly roll 1 scoop of ice cream at a time in cereal to coat. Place coated scoops of ice cream in ungreased jelly roll pan, 15 1/2 × 10 1/2 × 1 inch. Cover and freeze about 2 hours or until firm.

Set oven control to broil. Uncover pan. Broil scoops with tops 6 inches from heat about 30 seconds or until coating is light brown.

1 Serving: Calories 235 (Calories from Fat 90); Fat 10g (Saturated 5g); Cholesterol 30 mg; Sodium 220 mg; Carbohydrate 33g (Dietary Fiber 0g); Protein 3g

Easy Margarita Pie

8 SERVINGS

1 package (10 ounces) frozen strawberries in syrup, thawed

1 package (8 ounces) cream cheese, softened

1/2 cup frozen (thawed) margarita mix concentrate

1 container (4 ounces) frozen whipped topping, thawed

1 package (9 ounces) ready-to-use graham cracker pie crust

Place strawberries, cream cheese and margarita mix concentrate in blender or food processor. Cover and blend on medium speed until well blended. Pour mixture into medium bowl. Fold in whipped topping. Pour into pie crust.

Cover and freeze 4 to 6 hours or until firm. Let stand at room temperature 5 to 10 minutes before cutting. Cover and freeze any remaining pie.

1 Serving: Calories 355 (Calories from Fat 155); Fat 17g (Saturated 10g); Cholesterol 30 mg; Sodium 280 mg; Carbohydrate 46g (Dietary Fiber 1g); Protein 5g

DESSERTS WITH A MEXICAN ACCENT

The original Mexican dessert was simply the freshest local fruit at its peak: pineapple, oranges, strawberries, mangoes, papaya, bananas and melons, which grow in abundance and make a refreshing finale to a spicy meal.

With the introduction of sugarcane into Mexico, a variety of puddings, custards and pastries flavored with cinnamon, almond, caramel, fruit or cheese became popular. Invented or adapted from French and Spanish desserts, they were eaten in celebration of feast days.

Today, small servings are often served at the end of a meal and, more commonly, are eaten between meals. *Flan* (a custard-based dessert) is a nationwide favorite with recipes varying from region to region.

Oranges and Cinnamon

4 SERVINGS

4 chilled large seedless oranges, peeled and thinly sliced

1 teaspoon ground cinnamon

1/2 cup flaked or shredded coconut

Arrange oranges on serving platter or individual serving plates. Sprinkle with cinnamon and coconut.

1 Serving: Calories 95 (Calories from Fat 25); Fat 3g (Saturated 3g); Cholesterol 0 mg; Sodium 25 mg; Carbohydrate 20g (Dietary Fiber 4g); Protein 1g

Easy Mexican Chocolate Torte

8 SERVINGS

2 containers (8 ounces each) chocolate-flavored frozen whipped topping, thawed

Thirty-three 2 1/2-inch cinnamon graham cracker squares (about 2 packets)

Measure 4 cups whipped topping.* Place 1 tablespoon of whipped topping on 3 cracker squares; arrange crackers on serving plate, topping sides down, to form rectangle. Spread about 1/4 cup whipped topping over rectangle; top with 3 cracker squares. Repeat layers 9 times. Gently press torte together.

Using hands or pancake turners, carefully turn torte on its side so crackers are vertical. Frost top and sides with remaining whipped topping. Refrigerate 12 hours or overnight (crackers will completely soften and torte will become moist).

Each container of chocolate whipped topping contains 3 cups. Refrigerate remaining topping from second container for another use.

1 Serving: Calories 227 (Calories from Fat 100); Fat 11g (Saturated 9g); Cholesterol 2 mg; Sodium 180 mg; Carbohydrate 30g (Dietary Fiber 0g); Protein 2g

Mango Cream

6 SERVINGS

Easily prepared but festive in appearance, this fruit dessert offers interesting texture contrasts. To lower fat and calories, substitute low-fat frozen whipped topping for the whipping cream and sugar.

1 can (15 ounces) mangoes, drained and finely chopped (about 1 1/2 cups)

1 medium orange, peeled and chopped

1 cup whipping (heavy) cream

1/4 cup sugar

1/4 cup sliced almonds

6 maraschino cherries

2 tablespoons sliced almonds

Mix mangoes and orange in bowl; set aside. Beat whipping cream and sugar in chilled medium bowl until stiff. Fold mango mixture and 1/4 cup almonds into whipped cream.

Spoon mango mixture into 6 dessert dishes. Top each with 1 cherry. Sprinkle with 2 tablespoons almonds. Cover and refrigerate about 1 hour or until chilled. Garnish with mango slices, if desired.

1 Serving: Calories 240 (Calories from Fat 145); Fat 16g (Saturated 8g); Cholesterol 45 mg; Sodium 15 mg; Carbohydrate 25g (Dietary Fiber 3g); Protein 2g

Mango Cream

Flan

4 SERVINGS

1/2 cup sugar

3 eggs, slightly beaten

1 can (12 ounces) evaporated milk (1 2/3 cups)

1/3 cup sugar

2 teaspoons vanilla

1/8 teaspoon salt

Heat oven to 350°. Heat 1/2 cup sugar in heavy 1-quart saucepan over low heat, stirring constantly, until melted and golden brown. Divide sugar syrup among four 6-ounce custard cups; rotate cups to coat bottoms. Allow syrup to harden in cups about 5 minutes.

Mix remaining ingredients; pour into custard cups. Place cups in square pan, 9 × 9 × 2 inches, on oven rack. Pour very hot water into pan to within 1/2 inch of tops of cups. Bake 40 to 50 minutes or until knife inserted halfway between center and edge comes out clean. Immediately remove from water. Unmold and serve warm, or refrigerate up to 8 hours and unmold at serving time.

1 Serving: Calories 350 (Calories from Fat 100); Fat 11g (Saturated 6g); Cholesterol 190 mg; Sodium 210 mg; Carbohydrate 52g (Dietary Fiber 0g); Protein 11g

Toasted Bananas

6 SERVINGS

Here's a quick and easy dessert to serve with your favorite ice-cream topping.

3 firm, ripe medium bananas

2 tablespoons lemon juice

6 flour tortillas (8 or 10 inches in diameter)

1/4 cup sugar

3/4 teaspoon ground cinnamon

2 tablespoons margarine or butter, melted

1/3 cup chocolate, butterscotch or caramel ice-cream topping

Heat oven to 450°. Grease cookie sheet. Peel bananas and cut lengthwise in half; brush with lemon juice. Place 1 banana half on each tortilla. Mix sugar and cinnamon, reserving 1 tablespoon. Sprinkle bananas with sugar and cinnamon. Roll each tortilla around banana; place seam side down on cookie sheet. Brush with margarine. Sprinkle with reserved sugar and cinnamon.

Bake 6 to 8 minutes or until golden brown. Place on dessert plates. Drizzle with ice-cream topping. Serve with ice cream, if desired.

1 Serving: Calories 295 (Calories from Fat 65); Fat 7g (Saturated 2g); Cholesterol 0 mg; Sodium 270 mg; Carbohydrate 56g (Dietary Fiber 2g); Protein 4g

Toasted Bananas

Capirotada

6 SERVINGS

Mexican bread pudding has many variations, but always contains cheese and fruit.

3/4 cup packed brown sugar

1 teaspoon ground cinnamon

1 1/2 cups water

1 1/4 cups shredded Cheddar or Monterey Jack cheese (5 ounces)

2/3 cup raisins

1/3 cup slivered almonds

6 slices bread, toasted and broken into pieces (about 4 cups)

Heat oven to 350°. Grease 1 1/2-quart round casserole. Mix brown sugar and cinnamon in 1-quart saucepan. Stir in water. Heat to boiling, stirring occasionally. Boil uncovered 3 minutes, stirring occasionally. Mix cheese, raisins and almonds.

Spread one-third of the toast pieces in casserole. Sprinkle with one-third of the cheese mixture. Repeat layers twice. Pour sugar syrup over layers. Bake uncovered 20 to 25 minutes or until knife inserted 1 inch from edge comes out clean.

1 Serving: Calories 355 (Calories from Fat 110); Fat 12g (Saturated 6g); Cholesterol 25 mg; Sodium 290 mg; Carbohydrate 54g (Dietary Fiber 1g); Protein 9g

Peach Margaritas

6 SERVINGS (ABOUT 2/3 CUP EACH)

Cool off with a new margarita flavor—peach! For fun, dip the rims of the glasses into colored, coarse sugar.

1 lime, cut in half

Granulated sugar

3 cups crushed ice

1 cup tequila

2 tablespoons powdered sugar

1/2 can (12-ounce size) frozen peach juice concentrate, thawed

6 peach slices

Rub rims of 6 stemmed glasses with 1 lime half; dip rims of glasses into granulated sugar.

Squeeze juice from both lime halves into blender or food processor. Add remaining ingredients except peach slices to blender. Cover and blend on high speed until foamy. Pour into glasses. Garnish sides of glasses with peach slices. Serve immediately.

1 Serving: Calories 120 (Calories from Fat 0); Fat 0g (Saturated 0g); Cholesterol 0 mg; Sodium 2 mg; Carbohydrate 10g (Dietary Fiber 1g); Protein 0g

Peach Margaritas; Piñata (page 111); Strawberry-Lime Slush (page 110)

Strawberry-Lime Slush

4 SERVINGS (ABOUT 1 CUP EACH)

4 pints strawberries

3 cups crushed ice

1/2 cup powdered sugar

1/4 cup lime juice

Reserve 4 strawberries for garnish if desired. Place crushed ice and 2 pints strawberries in blender or food processor. Cover and blend on high speed about 30 seconds or until almost smooth, scraping down sides of blender container if necessary. Pour into 2-quart (or larger) pitcher.

Place remaining strawberries, the powdered sugar and lime juice in blender or food processor. Cover and blend on high speed about 30 seconds or until almost smooth. Pour mixture into pitcher; stir. Serve in 4 tall glasses. Garnish sides of glasses with reserved strawberries. Serve immediately.

1 Serving: Calories 75 (Calories from Fat 10); Fat 1g (Saturated 0g); Cholesterol 0 mg; Sodium 5 mg; Carbohydrate 18g (Dietary Fiber 2g); Protein 1g

Southwest Smoothie

3 SERVINGS (ABOUT 1 CUP EACH)

1/2 cup sliced banana

1/2 cup chopped mango, papaya or peach

2 cups milk

1 tablespoon honey

Place all ingredients in blender or food processor. Cover and blend on high speed until smooth. Strain if using mango. Serve immediately.

1 Serving: Calories 145 (Calories from Fat 25); Fat 3g (Saturated 2g); Cholesterol 10 mg; Sodium 80 mg; Carbohydrate 24g (Dietary Fiber 1g); Protein 6g

Fresh Fruit Frappé

7 SERVINGS (ABOUT 1 CUP EACH)

1 cup cut-up watermelon

1 cup cut-up cantaloupe or honeydew melon

1 cup cut-up pineapple

1 cup cut-up mango

1 cup strawberry halves

1 cup orange juice

1/4 cup sugar

Mix all ingredients in large bowl. Fill blender or food processor half full with fruit mixture; fill to top with crushed ice. Cover and blend on high speed until smooth. Repeat with remaining mixture. Serve immediately. Garnish with additional fruit if desired.

1 Serving: Calories 90 (Calories from Fat 0); Fat 0g (Saturated 0g); Cholesterol 0 mg; Sodium 5 mg; Carbohydrate 23g (Dietary Fiber 1g); Protein 1g

Fruit Flip

6 SERVINGS (ABOUT 1 1/2 CUPS EACH)

Coconut milk is thinner and less sweet than cream of coconut; don't confuse the two. Coconut milk is usually sold in the Asian-foods or canned-milk section of most large supermarkets.

1 can (14 ounces) coconut milk

2 cans (6 ounces each) pineapple juice

1 can (6 ounces) frozen orange juice concentrate

Place all ingredients in blender or food processor. Cover and blend on high speed about 30 seconds or until smooth. Pour over ice in glasses. Serve immediately.

1 Serving: Calories 215 (Calories from Fat 125); Fat 14g (Saturated 13g); Cholesterol 0 mg; Sodium 10 mg; Carbohydrate 20g (Dietary Fiber 0g); Protein 2g

Piñata

4 SERVINGS (ABOUT 1 1/2 CUPS EACH)

Cool drinks with lime juice and tropical fruits are popular in Mexico.

4 cups crushed ice

1 can (12 ounces) lime-flavored sparkling water, chilled

3/4 cup tequila or sparkling water

1/2 cup lime juice

2 medium bananas, peeled and broken into chunks

1/2 cup powdered sugar

Divide ice and sparkling water among 4 tall glasses. Place remaining ingredients in blender or food processor. Cover and blend on high speed about 30 seconds or until smooth. Pour into glasses; stir. Serve immediately.

1 Serving: Calories 210 (Calories from Fat 0); Fat 0g (Saturated 0g); Cholesterol 0 mg; Sodium 25 mg; Carbohydrate 30g (Dietary Fiber 1g); Protein 1g

Pineapple Limeade

8 SERVINGS (ABOUT 1 CUP EACH)

1/2 cup sugar

3 cups pineapple juice

1/2 cup lime juice

1 bottle (1 liter) sparkling water, chilled

Lime slices, if desired

Mix sugar, pineapple juice and lime juice in 3-quart pitcher. Refrigerate until chilled. Just before serving, stir in sparkling water. Serve over ice. Garnish with lime slices.

1 Serving: Calories 90 (Calories from Fat 0); Fat 0g (Saturated 0g); Cholesterol 0 mg; Sodium 5 mg; Carbohydrate 22g (Dietary Fiber 0g); Protein 0g

Beverages

Beer: The unique taste of beer is determined by what it is made from and how it is made. Beer is brewed from malted barley or other robust-flavored cereal grains such as rye or corn, and its slight bitterness comes from the dried flower of the hop plant. Yeast, used to create fermentation, provides the bubbles and frothy head beer is famous for. But one of the most important ingredients is the water, which accounts for 99 percent of its volume. Claims are often made by breweries that the quality and flavor of the water adds true character to its brew. And like wine, which has its chardonnays and cabernets, beer ranges in flavor, intensity and color with its lights, lagers, ales, porter and stout varieties.

Mexican beer or *cerveza* emerged as early as 1860, but its U.S. debut occurred in 1904 at the St. Louis World's Fair with a beer named Carta Blanca winning top prize. In the world of brewing beer, Mexico's industry is quite young, beginning after European immigrants, namely the German and Swiss, came to the country and shared brewing techniques. Export to the United States began with just a few brands in 1940, but surged with many new beers in the early 1980s. Of course, the popularity of Mexican restaurants increased familiarity of imported Mexican beers.

Beer is not only a terrific thirst quencher, it has the ability to put the fire out of hot and spicy foods due to its chemical makeup. Mexican beer is often served with a small wedge of lime.

Coffee: Coffee beans are grown in Mexico and exported worldwide, so it's no surprise that this is a popular drink. Mexican-style coffee is a rather sweet concoction of strongly brewed coffee with cinnamon and *piloncillo* (unrefined sugar) or brown sugar. Some versions of this drink include chocolate or cloves. Traditionally, this coffee is brewed in an earthenware pot or *olla,* but can be brewed in a saucepan or a drip-style coffee maker.

Fruit Drinks: The sun-drenched Mexican climate yields a plethora of succulent fruits having a multitude of culinary uses, but they are often found combined in cool and refreshing thirst quenchers. Big jars of blended drinks of fruit, water and ice called *frescas* add colorful merriment to the stands of outdoor vendors and markets. *Liquados,* another fruit-based drink, combine fruit, milk, ice and sugar.

Hot Chocolate: Cocoa beans and chocolate were introduced to Mexico by the Aztecs and were originally reserved for aristocrats, priests and nobles. But eventually chocolate became available to the population at large. The Aztec word for chocolate is *xoxolatl*, which means "bitter water." Mexican chocolate is usually found in tablet form and contains sugar, cinnamon, ground almonds and vanilla.

Kahlua: This coffee-flavored, dark brown liqueur is sweetened and is often added to hot coffee, served on the rocks with or without cream, or poured over vanilla ice cream for a simple, delicious dessert.

Margarita: Pale green margaritas, whether served over ice or frozen, provide instant recognition with Mexican cuisine. Tequila takes center stage in this tart-sweet cocktail, along with orange-flavored liqueur such as triple sec and lime juice. The rim of the margarita glass is usually dipped in lime juice and then in coarse salt. Apart from traditional lime, other fruit flavors, especially strawberry and peach, are also very popular.

Sangria: In Spanish, the word *sangria* means "bleeding," which denotes the dark red color of this wine-based beverage. Sangria is made from red wine, fruit juices, soda water and often brandy or orange liqueur. Sangria *blanco* is made with white wine. Occasionally, cinnamon sticks are used to add a spicy note. Sangria is quite refreshing and accompanies many dishes quite well.

Tequila: Probably the best known of all Mexican alcoholic drinks is the fermented sap of the agave plant (not the cactus as commonly thought), which thrives in arid, hot climates. The stem of the agave, known also as the "century plant," is used in making both *pulque* (another alcoholic beverage) and tequila. Tequila is pale and sharp-tasting and is available colorless or light gold. It is used in many cocktails but is also drunk in the classic way, accompanied by salt and lime.

Beverage Dress-up Ideas

Just a little attention to detail, whether an uncomplicated flourish of color, shape or texture, can make a simple food look spectacular and inviting. Garnishes aren't just for the dinner plate anymore. Dressing up your beverages adds tremendous appeal and fun and it is so easy to do using our suggestions below:

Easy Fruit Garnishes: Cut limes or lemons into small wedges and cut a small vertical slit in the wedge so it can be placed on the rim of the glass or bottle. Or, cut a small vertical slit in a whole strawberry and place on rim of glass. If desired, fruit garnishes can be floated in beverages. Garnishes can be prepared ahead of time; just cover and refrigerate until needed.

(Continued on next page)

Easy Salt or Sugar Rim: Rub glass rims with the cut side of a lime, lemon or orange then dip the rims into a shallow dish of coarse salt, as is traditional for margaritas, or sugar. Rims can be prepared up to eight hours ahead of time. Coarse salt, also known as margarita salt, is available in the beverage section of most large supermarkets or liquor stores. For an extra special and colorful touch, use red-, green-, yellow- or blue-colored sugar rather than plain white sugar. Colored sugar is available in the spice section of supermarkets.

Easy Frosted Glasses: Give your beverages a refreshing look by serving them in glasses that are frosted. Thoroughly chill the glasses in the freezer or refrigerator; remove just before serving and fill with completely chilled beverages.

Easy Ice Ideas: For perfectly clear ice cubes, use distilled water, which contains less of the minerals that cause cloudy ice. And, for drinks that won't taste "watered down," make ice cubes out of the beverage you are serving such as limeade, lemonade or iced tea. As the "ice cubes" melt, they won't dilute the flavor of the beverage. Note that alcoholic beverages or those that are very sugary will not freeze solidly.

Sangría

16 SERVINGS (1/2 CUP EACH)

1/2 cup brandy

1/2 cup orange-flavored liqueur

1/3 cup orange juice

1 bottle (4/5 quart) dry red wine, chilled

1 can (6 ounces) frozen lemonade concentrate, thawed

2 cups chilled ginger ale

Orange slices, if desired

Mix all ingredients except ginger ale and orange slices in 3-quart pitcher. Refrigerate until chilled. Just before serving, stir in ginger ale. Garnish with orange slices.

1 Serving: Calories 100 (Calories from Fat 0); Fat 0g (Saturated 0g); Cholesterol 0 mg; Sodium 10 mg; Carbohydrate 13g (Dietary Fiber 0g); Protein 0g

Mexican Coffee

5 SERVINGS (ABOUT 1 CUP EACH)

6 cups water

1/4 cup packed brown sugar

2 tablespoons ground cinnamon

2 whole cloves

1/2 cup regular grind coffee (dry)

1/4 cup chocolate-flavored syrup

1/2 teaspoon vanilla

Heat water, brown sugar, cinnamon and cloves to boiling in 3-quart saucepan, stirring to dissolve sugar. Stir in coffee; reduce heat to medium-low. Cover and simmer 5 minutes.

Stir in chocolate syrup and vanilla; remove from heat. Let stand 5 minutes for grounds to settle. Strain coffee into coffee server or individual cups; discard grounds mixture. Serve with whipped cream, if desired.

1 Serving: Calories 85 (Calories from Fat 0); Fat 0g (Saturated 0g); Cholesterol 0 mg; Sodium 20 mg; Carbohydrate 22g (Dietary Fiber 1g); Protein 0g

Glossary

Achiote Seed: The dried, reddish seeds of the annatto tree give food a bright orange-yellow tint when they have been cooked first in hot fat; the seeds themselves are discarded. Sometimes the seeds are ground to a powder and stirred into foods such as butter for color. They impart a flavor that is gentle and hard to describe; like that of saffron, it has an earthy quality.

Adobo: A piquant sauce of tomato, vinegar and spices.

Anise Seed: This small, elongated seed tastes sharply of licorice.

Avocado: See All About Avocados (page 97).

Beans: It takes time to prepare dried beans, but the result is a tender bean that is still firm. Canned beans may not be as firm as freshly cooked beans, but they are convenient and have just as much flavor. Dried beans keep almost indefinitely. Before cooking dried beans, rinse them well and pick them over for stones or dry, shriveled beans.

Black beans (*frijoles negros*, turtle beans) though small, have a hearty flavor. South American cooking makes great use of them. With their dramatic dark purple-blue color, they lend themselves nicely in combinations with yellow, red and orange colors.

Black-eyed peas (cowpeas) are the seeds of the cowpea, an annual vine. They are tan with a small black spot, which is the "black-eye."

Garbanzo beans (chickpeas) are Spanish in origin. These rounded, beige beans have a nutty flavor.

Great Northern beans are white, relatively large and mild.

Pinto beans (*frijoles*) are charmingly speckled with brown on a pale or pinkish background.

Red beans are favorites in the southern states. Pinto beans may be substituted.

Blue Cornmeal: Blue corn is another variety of field corn, but its kernels are dark blue to purple in color. When baked, the food is gray-blue to deep purple-blue in color. This variety is a staple in Mexico but has become more common in the United States in items such as tortilla chips and muffins. Unlike ordinary field corn, which can be eaten fresh, blue corn is always dried and ground before use.

Buffalo: This commercially raised red meat is similar in fat and cholesterol content to lean beef and tastes somewhat like beef; it does not have a gamy flavor. Buffalo meat is cut up the same as beef and can be prepared in the same manner, although it may dry out more quickly due to its lower fat content.

Capers: These are pickled, green buds from the prickly caper bush. They are somewhat smaller than raisins and are bottled in brine.

Cayenne: See Chile Primer (pages 16–18).

Chayote (christophine, mirliton, vegetable pear): Related to gourds, chayote squash have none of their brilliant decoration. Light green skin encases firm flesh of an even paler green. Chayote may be baked, steamed, stuffed or sautéed. A 1-pound chayote makes a nice serving for two or three people.

Cheese: Traditional Mexican cheeses were made with goat's or sheep's milk. Traditional Mexican cheeses may be difficult to find, but look for them in Hispanic or Latin markets or gourmet supermarkets.

Cheddar is a mild firm cheese of English origin that becomes sharper with age. It melts beautifully.

Chihuahua (Asadero or Oaxaca) is white, creamy and tangy. Sometimes it is sold braided. Mozzarella or Monterey Jack may be substituted.

Co-Jack is an American invention, a block cheese that marbles Colby and Monterey Jack.

Colby is a slightly sharp cheese with a flavor similar to that of Cheddar. This American cheese has a rather soft, open texture.

Monterey Jack is a mild cheese usually sold in blocks. It softens at room temperature.

Queso Añejo is an aged, hard grating cheese. It ranges from pale cream to white in color and is quite salty. Romano or Parmesan may be substituted.

Queso Fresco (*ranchero seco*) can be compared to a very salty farmer's cheese. A reasonable substitute for this crumbly cheese is feta.

Sierra is another rather dry, sharp cheese that grates easily. Romano or Parmesan may be substituted.

Chile: For descriptions of individual chilies see Chile Primer (page 16–18).

Chili Powder: See Chile Primer (page 16–18).

Chocolate: The Aztecs are credited with the discovery of chocolate. It was probably first used to flavor a bitter drink favored by mystics. Another Mexican invention, the *molinillo*, is a wooden whisk used to whip hot chocolate. The handle is rolled between the palms of the hands, whipping the mixture until it is frothy. Today, Mexican chocolate is usually found in tablet form and frequently contains cinnamon, vanilla, clove and ground almonds.

Chorizo: This spicy smoked pork (or pork and beef) sausage is available both in links and in bulk.

Cilantro (Mexican parsley, Chinese parsley, fresh coriander): This herb bears a resemblance to flat-leaf parsley, but the flavor is entirely different: strong, fresh and tangy. Cilantro is perishable; store it in the refrigerator with the stems in water and plastic loosely covering the leafy tops.

Cinnamon: This characteristic spice of Mexican cuisine is used in dishes both sweet and savory. It is available ground as a powder or in tightly rolled dry sticks.

Coriander: This spice is the seed of the plant that gives us cilantro. The plant is native to the Mediterranean and Asian countries but is commonly used in Indian, Mexican, Scandinavian and Caribbean cuisines. In Scandinavia, the ground seed is often used to flavor yeast breads, and ground coriander is an ingredient in curry powder. It may be purchased ground or as whole, dried seeds.

Corn Husks: Dried corn husks, softened by soaking, are used to wrap food before it is cooked. They make a sort of natural jacket that holds a mixture together as it steams.

Cornmeal: Dried corn is of course the staple of Mexican larders. When cornmeal is called for, use yellow or white, coarsely or finely ground.

Cumin: This is the powerful, sometimes dominating spice so often used in traditional Mexican cooking. Recipes may call for whole cumin seed or ground cumin.

Duck: This bird is considered "game" less and less, perhaps because it is widely available, frozen, in supermarkets. Wild duck tastes gamy, and in fact the flesh of waterfowl may take on a distinctly fishy flavor. Commercially raised ducks, though, are well fed, moist and have no gamy flavor.

Frijole: Spanish for "bean." See Beans (page 117).

Game: Americans tend to consider the following animals game: buffalo, duck, goose, pheasant, quail, rabbit and deer. Generally speaking, a farm-raised game animal hasn't had to scratch for a living and so is meatier and has a somewhat less gamy flavor. It is traditional to serve any game with the foods upon which it feeds. For example, serve game birds with berry sauces and wild rice.

Ground Red Pepper: See Cayenne chilies in Chile Primer (page 17).

Guava: These yellow-green fruits with pale faintly pink flesh are about the size of plums. They are intensely fragrant when ripe. The juice is often sold plain or blended with other fruit juices. Guava paste is only one of the fruit pastes found in Hispanic cuisine and it is often served with cream cheese as dessert. Guava paste is made by cooking the fruit with sugar until thick, then it is canned or shaped into blocks.

Hominy: These corn kernels have been soaked and lightly cooked so that the outer coating can be removed. Hominy is sold ready to use in cans in most supermarkets.

Instant Corn Flour Tortilla Mix (masa mix): This commercial product is the shortcut in making fresh corn tortillas.

Jerusalem Artichoke (sunchoke): This knobbed root keeps well in the refrigerator or other cold places. Jerusalem artichokes discolor after peeling so brush cut edges with lemon juice. Enjoy Jerusalem artichokes raw in salads, or broiled, stir-fried or mashed.

Jicama: See Jicama (page 85).

Juniper Berries: The fruit of an evergreen, juniper berries give gin its distinctive flavor. They are sometimes used to flavor game dishes. These blue-green berries are purchased dried. Add them (sparingly) whole to saucy foods for subtle flavor or slightly crushed for more impact.

Lard: This has been perhaps the most frequently used cooking fat south of the border since it was introduced by the Spaniards. For tender, flaky pastries, lard can't be beat. It is little known that lard, for all its reputation, has approximately half the cholesterol of butter.

Mango: The skin of this oval fruit is washed in gold, pink, red and parrot green. The flesh is deep yellow, juicy and richly perfumed. Mangoes have flat, oval pits. To slice the fruit, free it from pit in large pieces.

Masa: Its name literally means "dough" in Spanish. Masa is cornmeal dough made from dried corn kernels that have been softened in a lime (calcium hydroxide) solution, then ground. Masa is used to make corn tortillas.

Nopales: These leaves of the prickly pear (nopal) cactus are firm, crunchy pads. Let size be your guide in buying them; the smaller the pad, the more likely it is to be tender. Use tweezers to remove spines that haven't already been removed and a sharp paring knife or vegetable peeler to remove their bases. With a flavor similar to green beans, nopales are eaten both raw and cooked.

Nuts: In Mexican cooking, nuts are sometimes ground and stirred into sauces as a thickening agent. In addition to giving the sauce more body, nuts add their own particular flavor. Toasted nuts are more often used as a garnish or in baking. Toasting enhances the flavor of the nut.

- To Toast Nuts: Heat oven to 350°. Spread nuts in a single layer in an ungreased pan. Toast until light golden brown, stirring occasionally. Almonds, pecans and walnuts toast in 5 to 10 minutes and pine nuts toast in about 5 to 7 minutes.
- To Grind Nuts: Place 1/3 to 1/2 cup at a time in a food processor or blender. Cover and process them in short pulses *just until ground*. Continuous or overprocessing will cause nuts to form a sticky paste.

Papaya: A nearly oval fruit with creamy golden yellow skin, orange yellow flesh and scores of shiny black seeds conveniently packed in its center.

Pecan: This oil-rich nut is an American native. See Nuts (above) for toasting and grinding.

Pepita: See Pumpkin Seed (page 120).

Pepper: There is *Piper nigrum*, peppercorn, and then there's *Capsicum frutescens* and *Capsicum annuum*, the families of vegetables known as peppers and chilies. Peppercorns came to the Western world originally from Madagascar. The success of medieval spice traders made black pepper more widely available and only a little less precious than it had previously been.

Bell peppers are related to chilies but lack capsaicin (the compound that makes them hot). Bell peppers are therefore known as "sweet." Until recently, bell peppers of any color other than green were an oddity at many markets; today there are yellow, red and purple ones. Red and yellow are the sweetest in flavor. To roast bell peppers see page 18.

Pheasant: This game bird fares equally well when cooked with a bravely seasoned sauce or a mild, creamy one. Serve it with a grain side dish; see Game (page 118).

Piloncillo: This unrefined sugar is purchased in hard cones. Like other "raw" sugars, *piloncillo* is beige to brown; the deeper the color, the stronger the molasses flavor.

Pine Nuts (piñon, pignoli): Pine nuts are the seeds of the piñon pine. They are delicious raw or toasted. Store them tightly covered and either refrigerated or frozen depending on how quickly they are to be used. See Nuts (page 119), for toasting and grinding.

Plantain: This relative of the banana boasts a thick skin and large size. The fruit itself tends to be a deeper yellow than that of the banana. Cooked unripe, plantain is eaten as one would a potato. Plantains are sweetest when ripe, which isn't until their skins are thoroughly black. Like bananas, plantains will ripen after they have been harvested.

Posole: Sometimes hominy is called "posole," but the word authentically refers to a dish made with hominy as an ingredient. See Hominy (page 119).

Prickly Pear: This is the egg-size fruit of the cactus of the same name. It is nearly impossible to avoid the prickles when peeling to reveal the garnet-colored flesh. Prickly pears are sometimes sold with the prickles removed.

Pumpkin Seed: With the shells or husks removed, pumpkin seeds are known as *pepitas*. Store them in a cool, dry place. To toast pumpkin seeds, spread them in a single layer in an ungreased pan. Bake at 350° for 13 to 15 minutes, stirring and checking for doneness frequently, until light golden brown.

Quail: These little birds usually weigh in at about 1/4 pound. They have richly flavored meat, what there is of it. Quail are most commonly available frozen. See Game (page 118).

Queso: Spanish for "cheese."

Queso Añejo: The name means "aged cheese" in Spanish. See Cheese (pages 117–118).

Queso Fresco: The name means "fresh cheese." See Cheese (pages 117–118).

Rabbit: Rabbits are raised commercially. As with many uncommon meats, it is said of rabbit that it "tastes like chicken." It doesn't—it tastes like rabbit. Large rabbits aren't as tender as the little ones; it is well to marinate or stew older ones, or make rabbit sausage. See Game (page 118).

Red Pepper Sauce: This commercially bottled condiment is made from vinegar, spices and hot chilies. It adds heat but little in the way of flavor.

Rice: Mexican cooking calls for regular long grain or medium grain white rice.

Squash Blossoms: Despite popular belief, the blossoms used in Mexican cooking are those of winter squashes such as pumpkin, not zucchini. They are a perishable item and are best used the day they are bought.

Tamarind: This is an intensely pungent, tart pod about four inches long. Tamarind is usually bought packaged in a tightly compressed, sticky, plastic-wrapped lump. The flesh is riddled with fibers and seeds—not what you want in your food—and must be soaked before using. Separate the tamarind pods, pulling away and discarding as much of the pod as you reasonably can. Cover with water and let the pulp soak for at least an hour (overnight, if time permits). Then, squeeze the pulp well to extract the juice, or rub as much pulp as you can through a fine-mesh sieve.

Tequila: A pale, sharp-tasting liquor distilled from the agave plant, which thrives in an arid, hot climate. The stem of the agave, known also as the "century plant," is used in making both pulque and tequila.

Tomatillo: These fat little vegetables are the size of robust cherry tomatoes. They grow in papery husks reminiscent of Japanese lanterns and taste best when they are brilliant green in color. By the time they begin to turn yellow, they have lost some of their acidic freshness. This happens when they are lightly cooked too, but then, although they relinquish their vibrant color, they develop a gentler flavor and become more luscious. Uncooked, chopped tomatillos are the basis for chunky green salsas. Select tomatillos with their husks still drawn tightly around them. Husk and rinse off the sticky residue before using them.

Tomato: Roasting tomatoes gives them a faintly mysterious flavor. It works best with truly ripe, red tomatoes.

- To Roast and Peel Tomatoes: Set oven control to broil. Arrange cored tomatoes with their top surfaces about 5 inches from the heat. Broil, turning occasionally, until the skin is blistered and evenly browned, 5 to 8 minutes. The skins will be easy to remove. If the tomatoes are roasted on aluminum foil, clean-up will be easy and you'll be able to save any juice they give off as they roast.

Tortilla: Tortillas are round, flat unleavened breads made from ground wheat or corn. They are the basis of Mexican cookery. Tortillas are rolled, folded, used as dippers, fried crisp and munched fresh. Corn tortillas are cut into wedges and fried for chips. For the best chips, fry tortillas that are at least 1 day old. Flour tortillas, softer than those made from corn, are more popular in northern Mexico where corn does not flourish; wheat was brought there by the Spanish. Commercially made tortillas of both kinds are best stored in the freezer until needed.

Tripe: Usually what is meant by tripe is the lining of pig and sheep stomachs. Tripe is the identifying ingredient of traditional menudo, a hearty soup. Tripe needs to be thoroughly rinsed, often in three or four changes of cold water, before it can be used.

Venison: Venison is deer meat. Because it is lean, venison needs moist heat to keep it tender. See Game (page 118).

Walnuts: The flavor of this nut is delicious with corn. See Nuts (page 119), for toasting and grinding.

Metric Conversion Guide

Volume

U.S. Units	Canadian Metric	Australian Metric
1/4 teaspoon	1 mL	1 ml
1/2 teaspoon	2 mL	2 ml
1 teaspoon	5 mL	5 ml
1 tablespoon	15 mL	20 ml
1/4 cup	50 mL	60 ml
1/3 cup	75 mL	80 ml
1/2 cup	125 mL	125 ml
2/3 cup	150 mL	170 ml
3/4 cup	175 mL	190 ml
1 cup	250 mL	250 ml
1 quart	1 liter	1 liter
1 1/2 quarts	1.5 liters	1.5 liters
2 quarts	2 liters	2 liters
2 1/2 quarts	2.5 liters	2.5 liters
3 quarts	3 liters	3 liters
4 quarts	4 liters	4 liters

Weight

U.S. Units	Canadian Metric	Australian Metric
1 ounce	30 grams	30 grams
2 ounces	55 grams	60 grams
3 ounces	85 grams	90 grams
4 ounces (1/4 pound)	115 grams	125 grams
8 ounces (1/2 pound)	225 grams	225 grams
16 ounces (1 pound)	455 grams	500 grams
1 pound	455 grams	1/2 kilogram

Note: The recipes in this cookbook have not been developed or tested using metric measures. When converting recipes to metric, some variations in quality may be noted.

Measurements

Inches	Centimeters
1	2.5
2	5.0
3	7.5
4	10.0
5	12.5
6	15.0
7	17.5
8	20.5
9	23.0
10	25.5
11	28.0
12	30.5
13	33.0
14	35.5
15	38.0

Temperatures

Fahrenheit	Celsius
32°	0°
212°	100°
250°	120°
275°	140°
300°	150°
325°	160°
350°	180°
375°	190°
400°	200°
425°	220°
450°	230°
475°	240°
500°	260°

Helpful Nutrition and Cooking Information

Nutrition Guidelines:

We provide nutrition information for each recipe that includes calories, fat, cholesterol, sodium, carbohydrate, fiber and protein. Individual food choices can be based on this information.

Recommended intake for a daily diet of 2,000 calories as set by the Food and Drug Administration:

Total Fat	Less than 65 g
Saturated Fat	Less than 20g
Cholesterol	Less than 300mg
Sodium	Less than 2,400mg
Total Carbohydrate	300g
Dietary Fiber	25g

Criteria Used For Calculating Nutrition Information:

- The first ingredient is used wherever a choice is given (such as 1/3 cup sour cream or plain yogurt).

- The first ingredient amount is used wherever a range is given (such as 2 to 3 teaspoons milk).

- The first serving number is used wherever a range is given (such as 4 to 6 servings).

- "If desired" ingredients such as "2 tablespoons brown sugar if desired" and recipe variations are *not* included.

- Only the amount of a marinade or frying oil that is estimated to be absorbed by the food during preparation or cooking is calculated.

Cooking Terms Glossary:

Cooking has its own vocabulary just like many other creative activities. Here are some basic cooking terms to use as a handy reference.

Beat: Mix ingredients vigorously with spoon, fork, wire whisk, hand beater or electric mixer until smooth and uniform.

Blend: Mix ingredients with spoon, wire whisk or rubber scraper, until very smooth and uniform. A blender, hand blender or food processor can be used.

Boil: Heat liquid until bubbles rise continuously and break on the surface and steam is given off. For rolling boil, the bubbles form rapidly.

Chop: Cut into coarse or fine irregular pieces with a knife, food chopper, blender or food processor.

Crisp-tender: Doneness description of vegetables cooked until tender but still retaining some of the crisp texture of the raw food.

Cube: Cut into squares 1/2 inch or larger.

Dice: Cut into squares smaller than 1/2 inch.

Grate: Cut into tiny particles using small rough holes of grater (citrus peel or chocolate).

Grease: Rub the inside surface of a pan with shortening, using pastry brush, piece of waxed paper or paper towel, to prevent food from sticking during baking (as for some casseroles).

Julienne: Cut into thin, matchlike strips, using knife or food processor (vegetables, fruits, meats).

Mix: Combine ingredients in any way that distributes them evenly.

Sauté: Cook foods in hot oil or margarine over medium-high heat with frequent tossing and turning motion.

Shred: Cut into long thin pieces by rubbing food across the holes of a shredder, as for cheese, or by using a knife to slice very thinly, as for cabbage.

Simmer: Cook in liquid just below the boiling point on top of the stove; usually after reducing heat from a boil. Bubbles will rise slowly and break just below the surface.

Stir: Mix ingredients until uniform consistency. Stir once in a while for stirring occasionally, often for stirring frequently and continuously for stirring constantly.

Toss: Tumble ingredients lightly with a lifting motion (such as green salad), usually to coat evenly or mix with another food.

Ingredients Used in Recipe Testing:

- White rice is used wherever cooked rice is listed in the ingredients, unless otherwise indicated.

- Ingredients used for testing represent those that the majority of consumers use in their homes: large eggs, canned ready-to-use chicken broth, and vegetable oil spread containing *not less than 65% fat.*

- Fat-free, low-fat or low-sodium products are not used, unless otherwise indicated.

- Solid vegetable shortening (not butter, margarine, nonstick cooking sprays or vegetable oil spread as they can cause sticking problems) is used to grease pans, unless otherwise indicated.

Equipment Used in Recipe Testing:

We use equipment for testing that the majority of consumers use in their homes. If a specific piece of equipment (such as a wire whisk) is necessary for recipe success, it will be listed in the recipe.

- Cookware and bakeware *without* nonstick coatings are used, unless otherwise indicated.

- No dark colored, black or insulated bakeware is used.

- When a baking *pan* is specified in a recipe, a *metal* pan was used; a baking *dish* or pie *plate* means oven-proof glass was used.

- An electric hand mixer is used for mixing *only when mixer speeds are specified* in the recipe directions. When a mixer speed is not given, a spoon or fork was used.

Index

Numbers in *italics* refer to photos.